Further praise for Bri...

"Takes the reader on a thought provoking journey, filled with poignant observations, sound conclusions and practical advice. The hard hitting text will resonate with anyone who has dealt with the frustrating complexities of teenage turmoil."

> —DR. F. CRAIG SUDBURY, vice president of
> program development, Management and
> Training Corporation

"Clearly aimed at people who are out in the trenches dealing with teenagers, and well crafted to reach those people. It makes a great deal of sense."

> —DR. DONALD ARNSTINE,
> Professor Emeritus of Education,
> University of California–Davis, and author of
> *Democracy and the Arts of Schooling*

"A must read for anyone who knows a teenager in trouble or headed for trouble. The premise of the book is brilliant, and the suggested interventions are actual tools that work! We have purchased a copy for every employee in our company."

> —DR. JENNIFER WILD, president,
> Applied Technology Systems, Inc.

"It is definitely an eye opener and a useful tool for those of us who work with or have teenagers in our home or care on a daily basis."

> —BOOKER T. JONES, president and CEO,
> MINACT, Inc.

"I have a sixteen-year-old grandson I've raised. I'm using your techniques at home and he is responding. Thank you."

— D. H., San Antonio, Texas

"A great tool with great insight. There are not many people in America who would not benefit from reading this book."

— COL. HERBERT P. FRITTS (Retired),
director, Louisiana National Guard
Job Challenge Program

"A powerful book. I have a teenage daughter and the book is part of my must-have-toolkit now."

— M.K., Washington, DC

"Provides practical insight from the author's own experiences on the streets and his work with troubled youth. His writing [style] and extensive use of examples allow for easy reading and application of his advice."

— *YOUTH TODAY*: The Newpaper for
Youth Work

"Presents a compelling, sensible explanation of why and how young people make the choice between the street and the mainstream. More importantly, it presents a practical, effective strategy that positions adults to engage youth currently living the street life in a process that will guide them to become productive adults."

— KENNETH R. GINSBERG, MD,
associate professor of pediatrics,
Children's Hospital of Philadelphia,
author of *But I'm Almost 13*

BRING THEM BACK ALIVE

BRING THEM
BACK ALIVE

*Helping Teens Get
Out and Stay Out
of Trouble*

Jose M. de Olivares

3 1336 06735 2998

TAYLOR TRADE PUBLISHING

Lanham ■ New York ■ Dallas ■ Boulder ■ Toronto ■ Oxford

Published by Taylor Trade Publishing
An imprint of The Rowman & Littlefield Publishing Group, Inc.
4501 Forbes Boulevard, Suite 200
Lanham, Maryland 20706

Distributed by National Book Network

Library of Congress Cataloging-in-Publication Data

Olivares, Jose M. de, 1941–
    Bring them back alive : helping teens get out and stay out
of trouble / Jose M. de Olivares. — 1st Taylor Trade Pub. ed.
        p. cm.
    Includes bibliographical references.
    ISBN 1-58979-128-2 (pbk. : alk. paper)
    1. Problem youth—United States. 2. Problem youth—Behavior
modification—United States. I. Title.
HQ796.O39 2004
362.74'0973—dc22   2003024660

⊗™ The paper used in this publication meets the minimum requirements of American National Standard for Information Sciences—Permanence of Paper for Printed Library Materials, ANSI/NISO Z39.48–1992.
Manufactured in the United States of America.

To my son, Rod

Contents

Preface

I got in a lot of trouble when I was growing up in the South Bronx in New York City fifty years ago. But I was fortunate. There were adults around who cared about me and who knew what to do to help me straighten out my life. I have devoted that life to helping other teenagers straighten out their lives. I've worked in law enforcement, education, drug treatment and prevention, job training, and youth development in both the public and private sectors. I've successfully intervened in the lives of thousands of teenagers one-on-one, helped tens of thousands more teens through the programs I've developed and managed, and have had a positive impact on the lives of hundreds of thousands of teenagers through the local and national policies I've helped shape. I am writing this book to share my observations and my experiences with other adults who might be able to use this knowledge to help the teenagers in their lives.

This book is not a history of youth policy. It is not a critique of youth programs. I have not set out to prove a hypothesis. What I attempt to do is explain to you, the reader, why teenagers are getting in trouble in this country, because understanding why they get in trouble is essential to being able to help them get out of and stay out of trouble. That's what the first three chapters of the book are about. In chapters 4–7, I describe, with lots of practical examples, what you can do on an individual basis to help the teenagers in your family, or the teenagers you work with, straighten out their lives before they self-destruct. Chapter 8 deals specifically with the emotional hot buttons—gangs, drugs, and violence. Chapter 9 is a call to action.

You don't have to wait until the teenagers in your life are in serious trouble to read this book. If they are not behaving the way you think they should and you have not been able to get them to change their behavior, this book can help you. The strategy and the techniques I am going to share with you really do work. I know they work because I've lived them. They worked with me when I was growing up, they worked for me throughout my career helping teenagers, and they can work for you if you choose to use them.

I hope you do.

Troubled and Troublesome Teenagers

Are you concerned about the alarming number of teenagers who are quitting or being kicked out of school, getting pregnant, running away from home, stealing, using and selling drugs, becoming prostitutes, joining gangs, carrying guns, killing each other, or otherwise getting in trouble? If you care about the future of this country, you should be concerned. If you have children or grandchildren under the age of twenty, or work with young people that age, you'd better be concerned!

I was one of these teenagers when I was growing up in New York in the 1950s. We were called *juvenile delinquents* back then. That was the official label, but most adults called us hoods, short for hoodlums. The current label for these teenagers is *at-risk youth*. I happen to think that's a pretty stupid label, one that doesn't really tell me anything. At risk of what? If it's the risk of not growing up to be healthy, well-adjusted, productive citizens, every teenager in the country is probably at risk. If it's the risk of getting in trouble, what do you call these teenagers once they get in trouble? They are no longer at risk of getting in trouble once they are in trouble. And how old is a youth? Are preteens included? Are twenty-year-olds? Do you see my problem with the label? I've solved the problem by referring to teenagers who are getting in trouble as troubled and troublesome teenagers. I think that makes it pretty clear who I'm talking about.

While the labels we've chosen to describe teenagers who are getting in trouble have changed over the years, the teenage dropout problem, which is a euphemism for teenagers getting in trouble, really hasn't changed much since I was in my teens. It has just gotten bigger—a lot bigger! The U.S. Department of Labor's Bureau of Labor Statistics estimates that there are currently eleven million school-age youth who are not in school and don't have jobs. What else is there for these young people to do with all their time and energy except get in trouble? Add to that eleven million the unknown number of teenagers who are still in school or have jobs but may also be getting in trouble and it's easy to see why communities are frightened, parents are frantic, schools are overwhelmed, and politicians are overreacting.

Why is this happening? Why are so many teenagers dropping out? And what can be done?

You don't have to look far for answers to these questions. There are plenty of answers around. Everybody has a theory . . . and a program. The sociologists claim it is a family problem and can be solved by strengthening family ties. The psychologists argue it is a developmental phenomenon and propose more therapy and counseling. The oppressed see it as a consequence of injustice and demand equality. The righteous insist it is a reflection of moral decay in our society and urge a return to basic values. Left-wingers blame it on capitalism. Right-wingers say the courts are too soft. Parents point to the failure of schools. Teachers point to the failure of parents. Everybody blames the media. In fact, just about everything, from the nuclear arms race to rock and roll, has at one time or another been singled out as a cause of or a solution to the teenage dropout problem.

The trouble with all these theories is that they are just that—theories. There is probably some truth in all of them. And there is probably some value in the many programs they've spawned. It's just that the answers the theorists have given us aren't working. The problem isn't going away. Don't be fooled by reports that suggest a certain type of juvenile crime has gone down in a particular geographic area. You have to look at the big picture to understand the urgency of the situation. Yes, drive-by shootings and crack cocaine use are down in the inner cities, but schoolyard massacres and designer drug use are up in the suburbs.

Fortunately, there are some things that do work. There are people in this country who are making a real difference in the lives of teenagers. They actually prevent many teenagers from dropping out. Even more important, they bring back countless others who have dropped out. They know that programs don't change people's lives—people change people's lives; and they understand what it is teenagers need and want. They work with teenagers one-on-one to help them get what they need and want in a constructive and acceptable way. Their methods are replicable and they have been getting consistent results for decades. They come from all walks of life. They work with teenagers on a professional and voluntary basis or have teenage children of their own. They are teachers, counselors, coaches, social workers, ministers, youth workers, gang workers, police officers, probation officers, aunts, uncles, grandparents, and mothers and fathers. They remember what it felt like to be a teenager, they enjoy teenagers and they sincerely care what happens to teenagers.

I can imagine what you must be thinking about now: "If we know what works, why isn't everybody doing it?" That is a good question. I'm not sure I know the answer to it, but I'll tell you what I think. I think Pulitzer prize-winning author Harrison Salisbury got it right back in 1958 when he said in his book *The Shook-Up Generation*, "We lack the will."

The fact is, we really don't seem to like teenagers very much in this country. We love babies; they're so cute. And we love little children; there is so much to show them and do with them. We even like preteens, especially when they start acting and sounding like us. But as children mature they become less endearing. They begin to challenge adults. By the time they are teenagers we really don't want them around.

I always wondered why that was. Then one day I overheard a conversation that may have a lot to do with our attitude toward teenagers in this country. I was sitting in a booth in a Washington, D.C., restaurant and several European tourists were sitting in the booth behind me talking.

"They're so self-centered. I can't stand it. They think the whole world revolves around them."

"I know. And they're so impatient. They want everything and they want it all right now."

"What I can't stand is they have no sense of perspective, no appreciation for history or tradition. They always have to do everything their way. Nothing anybody else has ever done is good enough for them. They refuse to learn from anyone else's experience."

"Yes, and the worst part about it is they always think they're right and everyone else is wrong."

"I admit, they are very strong and energetic and creative, it's true, but I wish they weren't so obnoxious all the time."

"Ah-hah," I thought as I strained to listen, "These people are taking about my favorite subject, teenagers. Apparently they have the same problems with teenagers in Europe that we have here in the United States. This should be interesting." But they weren't talking about teenagers at all. They were talking about Americans . . . North Americans from the United States, to be exact.

That started me thinking. The fact is, we really are just an adolescent among nations. Two hundred and twenty five years or so of history as a nation isn't a lot of history. There are castles in Spain that took longer than that to build. Maybe our teenagers annoy us so much because they remind us of our own adolescent immaturity as a nation. Maybe that's why we don't want them around. Maybe that's why we lack the will to deal with them. Why else would adults in this country be so intolerant of teenagers when we were all once teenagers ourselves?

I could be wrong. It could be we're embarrassed to admit we don't understand our own kids; or we feel threatened by teenagers because they are younger, stronger, and possibly even smarter than we are. Whatever the reason, one thing is clear. There are too many adults in this country insisting they know what's best for teenagers and too few adults willing to really listen to what teenagers are saying they need and want. It's like the doctor telling the patient, "Never mind where it hurts. I'm the doctor. I know what's best." It would be ludicrous if it weren't so tragic.

It's time we stopped kidding ourselves. The millions of teenagers who are dropping out are dropping out of the labor force, the consumer marketplace, and the tax base. That's bad business, bad politics, and bad news. And if the economic impact of that loss isn't enough to get your attention, consider this. We pride ourselves on being the leaders of the free world. Well, who is going to follow us into the new century if we can't lead our own children into responsible adulthood?

I'm going to make some assumptions at this point. I've been told all my life I should never assume anything, but I'm going to anyway. First, I'm going to assume that, if you are reading this book, you are concerned about the troubled and troublesome teenagers in your family or in your community. I'm also going to assume that you have the will to help these teenagers straighten out their lives. Finally, I'm going to assume that you may not know exactly how to do that and could use some help.

I would like to help you by sharing what I have learned about helping teenagers—what I know works. I'm going to do that by answering three basic questions:

1. Where do teenagers go when they drop out?
2. Why do they go there?
3. What can you do to bring them back before they self-destruct?

The answers to these questions will provide you with a perspective, a frame of reference, that will help you understand why teenagers are dropping out in such alarming numbers. They will also provide you with a strategy and specific intervention techniques that you can use to help the teenagers in your life who are considering dropping out or have already dropped out.

I expect some of you will find my explanations and recommendations reassuring. They will confirm what you already know and do. Others will find them enlightening. They will provide insight and direction that will make you more effective in dealing with troubled and troublesome teenagers. Still others will disagree with me, especially with my explanation of where teenagers go when they drop out. However, once you get to the chapters on the strategy and intervention techniques you can use to help troubled and troublesome teenagers straighten out their lives, I believe it will all begin to come together and make sense to you.

I say this with some confidence because, for the past twenty years, I have been teaching the material I am about to share with you to people who work with teenagers all across the country and have seen them react to the material in these ways. In fact, it is at the urging of the people I've taught that I started writing this book. So, if you find yourself in that group that is having difficulty accepting my initial explanations, I ask you to temporarily suspend disbelief. I ask you to accept my explanations, at least until you've had the chance to see where they lead. If, after you finish reading the book, you still disagree with me, that's okay. It's really all about the bottom line, anyway. If the way you are dealing with teenagers is working to your satisfaction, then by all means keep dealing with them that way. If, on the other hand, you are not getting the results you want in your dealings with teenagers, maybe it's time to change what you're doing.

I'm not going to promise that once you follow the recommendations in this book, you will be able to prevent every teenager from dropping out. The factors that contribute to a teenager's dropping out are very complex and often beyond the control of any one person. I will assure you, however, that if you follow these recommendations, you will be able to bring most of those who do drop out back alive.

2

Crossing the Line

A popular misconception about the United States is that it is one big society divided into numerous subgroups, all of which are stacked on top of each other like a pile of bricks. These subgroups overlap in some places, stick out in others, with each group trying to get to the top of the pile. While it is true that we have divided ourselves into many subgroups (by race or ethnicity, geography, economics, education, occupation, age, gender, etc.) and we have stacked these groups in a pile one on top of the other, the United States is *not* one big society. It is two societies, two very different societies that are separated by the fundamental principle on which the nation was founded—the principle of law.

I call one of these societies *the mainstream*. The mainstream in this country is a society based on the belief that, "all men are created equal, and are endowed by their Creator with certain inalienable Rights." It was a pretty radical belief when Thomas Jefferson wrote it into the Declaration of Independence a couple of hundred years ago. Prior to that time, most societies believed that some men were endowed with more rights than others by reason of their physical strength or their parentage. Jefferson and his friends changed all that with the stroke of a pen and the blood of a revolution. We continue to "hold these truths to be self-evident." Admittedly, it has taken us a while to clarify that the word "men" means men and women of all races, creeds, and economic backgrounds, but we have made considerable progress in that direction.

The mainstream in the United States today is defined, as it has always been defined, by the Constitution. It is a society of laws, laws that are intended to guarantee every citizen the opportunity to pursue his or her dreams and provide every citizen with a safe and secure future in which to pursue those dreams. We don't all have the same dreams in the mainstream, the same plans for the future, but whatever it is we strive for we call it success. The mainstream is a law-abiding, success-oriented society.

Unfortunately, not everyone in this country "hold[s] these truths to be self-evident." There are a great many people living in the United States who, for a variety of reasons, believe in another order—the natural order. They believe in survival of the fittest. The way they see it, it is a dog-eat-dog world, and there are no guarantees. They call their society *the street*. It is a survival-oriented society that exists without regard for the mainstream's laws.

Keep in mind there are many uses for the words "mainstream" and "street." I am using them here in a very specific way. I am not using "mainstream" to describe a dominant moral code or set of cultural norms. And I am not using "street" to describe homeless people who literally live on the street because they have nowhere else to live. I'm also not using "street" to describe the Wall Street business community, which is often referred to as The Street. When I talk about living in the mainstream, I am talking about people who live within the laws of the land. When I talk about being on the street, I am talking about people who live without regard for those laws.

According to Abraham Maslow's Hierarchy of Human Needs, all human beings have the same needs. We all need water, food, clothing, shelter, safety and security, love and affection, self-esteem, and self-actualization—in that order. While we may not all be attempting to meet the same level of need at a given moment, sooner or later we all need the same things whether we live in the mainstream society or the street society. In addition to the things we need, there are the things we want. We usually want what we need, but we don't always need what we want so we don't all want the same things. The Rolling Stones probably described the relationship between needs and wants best when they said, "You can't always get what you want, but if you try sometimes, you might find, you get what you need."

Whatever it is we need or want, it is available in both the mainstream and street societies. The point is, if we pursue our needs and wants within the framework of the mainstream's laws, those laws protect what we get. We can keep what we earn in the mainstream until we die. Even then, we can leave what we have acquired or achieved to our heirs. It is not so on the street. You can get anything on the street you can get in the mainstream. The law just doesn't protect it; consequently, you can only keep it until someone stronger takes it away from you.

When we talk about the teenage dropout problem what we are really talking about is teenagers dropping out of the mainstream society and joining the street society.

But where exactly is the street society? Do you know where to find it?

Both the street society and the mainstream society in the United States exist in the same time and space. There is no tangible border between the two societies with signs telling you when you've left one and entered the other. In fact, the line between the two societies can be so subtle that, without a thorough understanding of it, you may not be able to see it or tell one side from the other.

The line that separates the street from the mainstream has four characteristics that you must understand in order to find it:

1. It runs vertically.
2. It has teeth.
3. It is invisible.
4. It moves.

The Line Runs Vertically

To begin with, the line runs vertically, not horizontally. Remember the subgroups I mentioned earlier that are stacked on top of one another? Well, the line that separates the street from the mainstream doesn't run horizontal to that stack, slipping between the subgroups at some point separating them into an upper and lower tier. It runs vertically through the whole stack, cutting through each and every subgroup. The position of the line is not determined by race or ethnicity, geography, economics, education, occupation, age, or gender. It is determined by the law.

People living on the street tend to have little difficulty understanding this characteristic. People living in the mainstream, on the other hand, often miss the point. Mainstream people, including many government officials and scholars who should know better, tend to equate minorities, the inner cities, and poor folks with the street, and whites, suburbia, and middle-class folks with the mainstream. That is a terrible mistake. The line between the street and the mainstream has nothing to do with the color of a person's skin or a person's cultural heritage. People of all races and ethnic backgrounds live within the law and people of all races and ethnic backgrounds live without regard for the law.

The line has nothing to do with geography, either, with urban and rural or with "the right side of the tracks" and "the wrong side of the tracks." Some neighborhoods may have a greater proportion of mainstream or street people living in them, but no neighborhood is the exclusive domain of either society. For example, the heads of organized crime families in this country may live down the block from the presidents of major corporations, but having a fancy house in a fancy neighborhood doesn't make the crime bosses mainstream. And a law-abiding, single mother, struggling to feed her children with public assistance payments and attending job-training programs to try to get off the welfare rolls, may live down the hall from drug dealers in the public housing projects. But living next door to drug dealers doesn't make the law-abiding, single mother a street person. It is people's actions that determine which society they belong to, not their addresses.

As for wealth, education, or any of the other factors that contribute to socioeconomic status, forget about them. Socioeconomic status doesn't determine whether a person is a member of the street or mainstream society. Socioeconomic status is just a tool, a powerful tool, but a tool nonetheless. Mainstream people use it to become more successful. Street people use it to survive more easily. Wealthy, socially prominent people who break the law are less likely to get caught than people with lower socio-economic status because they aren't being watched as closely; and if they do get caught they can afford the best lawyers to defend them. But the son of a doctor who forges his father's prescriptions is no less of a criminal than the drug dealer he sells them to.

Don't confuse Marx's "class struggle" with the street and the mainstream in the United States. Of course the "have nots" are going to try to get what the "haves" have, and the "haves" are going to try to keep them from getting it. That's not the issue. The issue is how the "haves" and the "have nots" go about achieving their ends. If they operate within the law they are part of the mainstream society. If they break the law to get what they need and want or to keep what they have, they are part of the street society.

While I am on the subject of class, I should point out that there is no such thing as white-collar crime. The notion that there are degrees of crime, and that white-collar crime is somehow less offensive or threatening to the mainstream than blue-collar crime is a scam invented by street people to trick the mainstream into looking the other way. This form of hiding behind respectability is a very old and a very basic scam but an effective one. "Drug dealers are trying to corrupt our children," proclaims the pension fund administrator. "We must stop them before it's too late," he urges. Then, as you focus your attention on the drug dealers, the pension fund administrator quietly embezzles a couple of million dollars of your retirement money.

Hiding behind respectability is a scam teenagers use as well. It is especially popular among siblings. It is not unusual, for example, to find the quiet, obedient, apparently considerate daughter secretly provoking, and then calling attention to, her more outspoken, rebellious, self-involved sister to draw her parents' attention away from her own illegal activities. Don't be fooled. Crime is crime. Breaking the law is breaking the law and it takes you out of the mainstream and puts you on the street no matter who you are or where you are.

You cannot distinguish mainstream people from street people by the way they look, where they live, how much money or education they have, by their occupation, age, or gender. The line that separates them is the law. If you don't understand that, you are doomed to wrongfully suspect innocent people of being criminals and be completely oblivious to criminal activity going on right under your nose.

Having said that, I need to acknowledge that many people will argue that the single mother on welfare I talked about earlier will not be perceived as a member of the mainstream, even though she is, because she is poor, or not well educated, or a person of color, or living in a housing project. They will further argue that the reality is, because she is not perceived as mainstream, she will not be protected by the law as are other mainstream people. Good point. Hold that thought. I'll get back to it in a moment.

The Line Has Teeth

The second important characteristic of the line is that it has teeth and they only point one way. Mainstream people don't want street people around. If street people are citizens, and most of them are, the mainstream can't keep them out of the country, but the mainstream has gone to great lengths to protect itself from people who do not respect its laws. It has created an elaborate system to identify street people and isolate them so they cannot pose a threat to the people who live in the mainstream.

That system consists of the police, the courts, and the jails. Together they are called the criminal justice system.

To be precise, a jail is where you are kept while your case goes to trial or where you are sentenced for lesser crimes. Jails are run by cities and counties. A prison is where you serve your sentence if found guilty of a serious crime. Prisons are run by states and the federal government. I'm going to call them all jails—meaning locked up.

It is extremely important to understand that the criminal justice system doesn't work for all Americans. It works for the mainstream society and it works against the street society. That is not a flaw in the system. That is the way it was designed. If you tried to picture it, it would look like the treadles around a parking lot. The teeth point one way. You can cross from the mainstream to the street anytime, but you can't come back to the mainstream without paying a price and that price is your liberty.

Let me give you an example.

Suppose you're planning a party and you go to the local liquor store to buy a case of wine that sells for $100. The clerk takes your $100 but only gives you half a case of wine. When you complain, the clerk pulls a gun out from behind the counter and threatens to shoot you if you don't get out of the store. What would you do (after you leave the store, that is?)? Call the police, of course. The clerk has broken two laws. He has stolen your money and threatened you with a gun. And the police would come and intercede on your behalf. The clerk would be arrested, given a trial and, if found guilty, put in jail—and you'd probably get your money back.

Now imagine that your drug of preference is cocaine, an illegal as opposed to a legal drug. You go to your local drug dealer to buy $100 worth of cocaine for your party. The dealer takes your $100 but only gives you half the amount of cocaine you paid for. When you complain he pulls a gun and threatens to shoot you if you don't "get outta my face." Now what would you do? Would you call the police? I doubt it. If you did, the police would arrest you along with the drug dealer because buying drugs is just as illegal as selling them. You can't risk asking the police to intercede on your behalf. You'd be out $50. Of course, you could get a gun of your own and try to take back your money, but then you'd run the risk of getting shot or getting caught and going to jail.

Let me give you another example. This point is too important to pass over lightly.

Let's say you steal $1,000 from your employer and you use the money to buy a fancy stereo. One day, several months later, you come home and find your house has been burglarized and your stereo has been stolen. Would you call the police? You could, but you'd run the risk that, in the course of their investigation, the police would find out you stole the money to buy the stereo and arrest you. You'd have to stand trial, and if found guilty, you could go to jail. Chances are you wouldn't want to take that risk.

What was that you said? Did you say the police could never prove you stole the money you used to buy the stereo? That's how a street person thinks. Maybe you're right and they can't prove it . . . but then again, maybe they can. The point is, if you hadn't stolen the money in the first place there would be nothing to prove. You see, you gamble with your liberty when you step across the line from the mainstream to the street. Those are pretty high stakes. And what are the odds of getting caught? None of the people in jail today thought they'd get caught.

Keep in mind the mainstream is very, very serious about protecting itself from people who don't respect its laws. It is so serious, in fact, that it gives the people it hires to operate the criminal justice system more power than it gives to any other citizen in the country. It gives them the power to search and seize, to question and detain, to incarcerate, even to take life. For instance, no one in this country is allowed to take the life of another person for any reason other than self-defense. No one. Not even the president of the United States. No one, except members of the criminal justice system. Police officers are allowed to shoot a fleeing felon, judges in many states can sentence convicted murderers to death, and corrections officers are allowed to shoot inmates attempting to escape from jail. That's a lot of power.

Of course, the mainstream doesn't want the criminal justice system to abuse the power it has been given, so it has limited the use of that power through something called due process, which is spelled out in the Bill of Rights. If the members of the criminal justice system violate due process in a specific instance, they lose their power in that instance. If a police officer improperly obtains evidence it cannot be used in court. If a judge exceeds his or her authority in a particular trial the verdict can be overturned. If a jail does not have enough space to house its prisoners under humane conditions it must release some of those prisoners . . . and so on.

There is a running battle in this country over how many limitations need to be placed on the criminal justice system to keep it from abusing its power, and how many limitations can be placed on it before it loses its ability to do its job. The question of how much due process is enough tends to swing back and forth like a pendulum between the right of the mainstream to protect itself as a society, a right given it by the Constitution, and the rights of individual members of the mainstream guaranteed them by the Bill of Rights.

Now, back to the single mother on welfare who is a mainstream person but may be perceived and treated as a street person. Does that actually happen? Of course it does, and a lot more often than we'd like to think. My point is that it doesn't happen because the system is unfair. It happens because some of the people who work for the criminal justice system, and some of the mainstream communities they serve, don't understand or choose to acknowledge the first characteristic of the line that separates the street from the mainstream. They keep trying to run the line horizontally, between subgroups, instead of vertically through all the different subgroups. The result of their ignorance is injustice on the one hand, ineffectiveness on the other. When a community and its criminal justice system use criteria other than the law to decide who is on the street and who is in the mainstream one of two things happens: they either wind up pursuing people they perceive to be on the street who are really in the mainstream, like our single welfare mother, which is unjust; or they overlook people they perceive to be in the mainstream who are really on the street, which is ineffective.

I was a police officer early in my career and, as a result of that intense experience, I have a strong appreciation for and understanding of the criminal justice system. It serves the wishes of its community. So don't blame cops, judges, or wardens for injustice or ineffectiveness. Educate them. Let them know exactly how far you want them to go in order to protect you. Let them know where the threat to the mainstream, the threat to your safety and your future, is coming from. It is coming from the people who live without regard for the mainstream's laws. It is coming from the street. Nobody else is a threat. Nobody else should be treated as a threat.

If you happen to be one of those street people I've been talking about, one of those people who lives without regard for the mainstream's laws, make no mistake about it, the mainstream is out to get you. The cop is the dog-catcher in the dog-eat-dog world. If another street person doesn't get you, the mainstream will. You can try to "get over," learn to "deal with the man," maybe even "beat the rap" now and then. You can survive today and possibly tomorrow, but sooner or later the road will run out and you'll drive over those treadles I talked about and be trapped because the street is a dead end.

The Line Is Invisible

The third characteristic of the line that separates the mainstream society from the street society is that it is invisible. It is shrouded in language the way a country road is veiled by the morning fog—shrouded in loopholes, precedents, and rules.

Loopholes are what laws don't say. For example, you and I are in a room together. I want to keep you from getting to my side of the room. So, I draw a line on the floor and make a law saying you can't cross it. If you step over my line, you have broken the law and will go to jail. But if you go out the door behind you, come around the building and come in the window behind me, you will be on my side of the room, which is what my law was intended to prevent, but you haven't actually broken the law. And I can't put you in jail. It may appear as though you have broken the law, but you have only violated the intent of the law, not the letter of the law. The mainstream doesn't hold people accountable for what it intends, only for what it says. Are you still a mainstream person if you use a loophole? Absolutely!

If loopholes are about what laws don't say, precedents are about what laws mean. Laws are made up of words and words often have more than one meaning. The meaning of the words in a law is subject to the interpretation of a judge every time the law is challenged (every time someone is charged with breaking that law). For example, most states have a law that says you can't distribute pornographic material. But what is pornographic material? I may think a picture of a naked lady is pornographic. You could contend that it is a work of art. If a previous interpretation of the word pornographic, if the precedent, supports your contention, then you haven't broken the law, even though it may appear to me that you have. And I can't put you in jail.

Then there are rules. Rules are the most difficult part of the shroud to penetrate. Rules pertain to things the mainstream says people should not do, as opposed to things it says they must not do. That sounds simple enough. What complicates matters is that we don't uniformly call the things you should not do rules and the things you must not do laws. We use the two words almost interchangeably. And we use a lot of other words, as well, to describe what you should not and must not do . . . like regulations, ordinances, misdemeanors, and felonies. It can get pretty confusing. What you need to remember in order to distinguish between rules and laws is that rules limit or regulate behavior that is objectionable while laws prohibit behavior that is considered sufficiently threatening to warrant excluding violators from the society that made those laws. You don't lose your status or privileges as a member of the mainstream for breaking a mainstream rule. You do lose your status and privileges as a member of the mainstream for breaking a mainstream law.

Take a city ordinance that says you can't park in front of a fire hydrant and carries a fine of $50. It is a city rule. What it is really saying is, you can park in front of a fire hydrant in the city if you are willing to pay $50. Compare that with a state law that says you can't steal someone else's car and carries a two to five year jail sentence as a penalty. That's a real law. What it says is, if you steal a car and you get caught, you will lose your status and privileges as a citizen of that state for a minimum of two years.

Here's another example.

Schools have all sorts of rules that govern student behavior. One of them invariably deals with truancy. If you cut classes you may be required to stay after school for several days or have your parents come in for a conference. That's a real rule. On the other hand, if you strike a teacher you will be expelled. Now obviously, being expelled from school is not the same as going to jail. But from the schools point of view, it has the same effect. Expelling you from school excludes you from the school population and causes you to lose your status and privileges as a student. That makes the prohibition against striking a teacher a school law, as opposed to a school rule, even though it is called a school rule.

I know the distinction I am making between rules and laws may sound picky, but it is an important distinction because breaking a rule doesn't put you across the line that separates the street and the mainstream. Only breaking a law, a law that excludes you from the society that made the law, does that.

Taking advantage of loopholes and legal precedents or breaking rules to get what you need or want is acceptable mainstream behavior that looks like street behavior. That's what makes the line between the two societies so fuzzy—so hard to see. The problem with operating so close to the line is that it is risky. It's just like driving down that country road in the fog. You'll probably get where you want to go, but the chances of missing a turn or running off the road are much greater in the fog than if you drive the same road on a clear day. There is also a risk of being run into by another car when you're driving in the fog.

Taking the fog analogy one step further, the better you know the road, the better your chances of getting where you want to go in the fog. If you don't know the road, you probably should take someone along with you who does. The same holds true when you operate close to the line between the street and the mainstream. The better educated you are, the better you know the road. The best educated person when it comes to the line between the street and the mainstream, the person you want to take along with you if you are going to operate close to that line, is a lawyer. And, of course, that is exactly what people do. They hire the best lawyer they can afford to guide them so they can get as close to the line as possible without actually crossing over it. Sometimes they get away with it. Sometimes they don't and they wind up across the line. We hear about it every day in the news media. A respected public official accepts a favor from a grateful constituent and winds up being accused of taking a bribe. A successful businessman is looking for a creative way to finance the purchase of new equipment and finds himself indicted for laundering drug money. The fog always leaves wrecks on the side of the road.

This shroud that covers the line between the street and the mainstream poses a special problem for teenagers. That is because this gray area I have been talking about doesn't really exist for them. The mainstream operates on a double standard when it comes to teenagers. It has created something called a status offense. A status offense is a catchall that makes it illegal for teenagers not to do as they are told. An adult can run out on his or her family, not go to work, have sex with a consenting adult and not face the threat of imprisonment. There are consequences for such behavior; there may be rules that regulate it and a price to pay for doing it, but it is not prohibited by law. Adults won't go to jail for operating in the gray area. Teenagers, on the other hand, don't have that luxury. If they run away from home, don't go to school, have sex with a consenting teenager, or just plain don't listen to their parents, they are guilty of a status offense and can be deprived of their liberty. The significance of this fact is that certain behavior that might fall into the gray area for an adult and, therefore, still be legal and considered mainstream, will be illegal for teenagers and will put them across the line and on the street.

The Line Moves

The fourth important characteristic of the line is that it moves. There are two reasons for this. One reason is laws can be changed and are changed. The second reason is not all laws are made by the same people. The mainstream has divided itself into various jurisdictions of government, each subject to the jurisdiction above it, but each having authority to make its own laws governing its own section of the larger mainstream society. In addition to the federal government, states, counties, cities, municipalities, school districts, corporations, even associations can and do make their own laws and can exclude people who break those laws from participating in their section of the mainstream. We saw how that worked in the school example earlier. With so many different governing bodies making laws, the laws are bound to vary from one jurisdiction to another.

For example, in one state possession of a small quantity of marijuana may be a misdemeanor with a small fine as a penalty and prostitution may be a felony with serious jail time attached. Across the border, in the very next state, the exact opposite might be the case. Possession of even a small quantity of marijuana may be a felony carrying serious jail time as a penalty, while prostitution may be regulated and carry a small fine if you don't have the required health certificate.

In effect, each legally constituted entity has a say in defining where the line will be drawn in its jurisdiction; further, the citizens within each jurisdiction have the right, through the process of representative democracy, to change the law, abolish it, or make a new one. It is a creative way of accommodating differences, but it can, and often does, lead to confusion and create inequities. You have to know what jurisdiction you are in and what laws are in effect at the time in order to know where the line is.

This is probably a good place to deflate another popular myth about laws. A lot of people believe that the street has its own code of behavior. They believe that street people obey that code much the way mainstream people obey the Code of Criminal Justice. That couldn't be further from the truth. If you share that notion, get it out of your head. The street and the mainstream are as dissimilar as they can be precisely because the street, as a society, has no laws and the mainstream is based on law. It is true that street people will tell you, "You never drop a dime on the street because snitches get stitches," as if that were part of some code of behavior. What they are really saying is, if you inform on someone on the street that person will probably try to hurt you. If you are afraid of that person you might choose not to inform on him or her. If you aren't afraid of that person, and informing on him or her would help you survive, you would give that person up in a New York minute. Think about it. If street people lived by this supposed code and didn't inform on other street people, how could every police office in the country have dozens of informants . . . which they do?

Individuals on the street, or groups of individuals, can and do tell other people what to do. And these same individuals can and do make other people do what they've been told. They do it by force, intimidation, guile, deceit, or whatever means are available to them. But there is no agreed upon code of behavior on the street, nor is there a system to apprehend, judge, and exclude anyone from the street for unacceptable behavior. It's all about personal survival. You do whatever you can get away with doing to meet your needs and wants.

One final thought about the law—the line that separates the street and the mainstream. One would hope that the people who make laws, the legislative bodies of the various jurisdictions, would take moral and ethical considerations into account when making laws, and they usually do. Some of the greatest debates in the history of the United States have been among lawmakers arguing the moral or ethical considerations of a proposed law. However, it is not required. Determining what is moral or ethical is not the purpose of law. Those are personal standards you set for yourself. The law does not define good and evil. It does not determine what is right or wrong. In fact, by separating church and state, the law specifically guarantees you the right to decide for yourself what is good or evil and what is right or wrong. The law defines the behavior the legislators in a particular jurisdiction have chosen to allow or not allow. That's all it does. If you think I'm acting unethically or immorally you don't have to associate with me, but you can't exclude me from the mainstream or deny me the privileges I am entitled to as a member of the mainstream if I don't break the law. And if I do break the law, I will subject myself to the realities of the street and be pursued by the criminal justice system regardless of whether you or I believe my actions are justifiable on moral or ethical grounds.

In this respect, neither the street nor the mainstream is intrinsically good or evil. The two societies represent fundamentally different worldviews. Each reflects a value system that is different from and incompatible with the other. And as the popular singer Willie Nelson so aptly put it, "Different ain't better, just different." Both societies provide opportunities for people to get what they need and want. The compelling argument for living within the mainstream's laws is that, if you do, you can enjoy the privileges and protection those laws afford. You can keep what you get in the mainstream.

So now you know where teenagers go when they drop out of the mainstream. They go to the street. And you know where the street is—everywhere. But do you really understand what it means to be on the street? Do you know what it's like to live in the street society?

It means your future is no longer protected, so planning for a future makes no sense. Success, however we define it in the mainstream, is a nonexistent concept on the street. There is no tomorrow on the street. There is only today. You get what you need and want and hold on to it any way you can, one day at a time, for as long as you can.

It means the institutions and officials that protect the mainstream don't protect you. Quite the contrary, they are your mortal enemies. They are to be avoided, outsmarted, and even overpowered if possible. They are never to be trusted because they will hurt you by depriving you of your liberty every chance they get.

It means you can never show weakness because if you do you will become prey for everyone else on the street. You especially must respond to every physical threat and every attempt at intimidation with equal or superior physical force. If you don't, you will surely be a victim of others' violence.

It means you can't care about anyone or anything but yourself. You can't afford to feel sympathy or compassion because it will make you soft, and being soft can get you killed.

It means you are on your own. Sure, you can make friends on the street, have a family, even band together with other street people to pursue shared needs. You just can't trust relationships with street people. When it comes down to their needs or your needs, their going to jail or your going to jail, their being hurt or your being hurt, they will sell you out in a heartbeat. There is no "honor among thieves."

It also means you can't go back to the mainstream without paying a price and that price is your liberty. You might, under some circumstances, be able to slip back to the mainstream before anyone notices you've left, but you will still have the threat of being caught for something you did on the street hanging over you.

And finally, although you may not realize it, it means sooner or later you are going to wind up dead or in jail because the street is a dead end.

Can you imagine what living that way must feel like? Let me help you. Have you ever inadvertently run a stop sign while you were out driving? Do you remember how you felt the instant you realized what had happened? What was the first thing you did? Exactly, checked the rearview mirror. Can you remember how you felt at that precise moment? Think about it for a second. Get in touch with that feeling. It isn't very pleasant, is it? That's what living on the street feels like all the time.

That's the downside. However, as cruel and as frightening a society as the street may be, it is not without redeeming qualities. It has an allure, an excitement, and an intensity about it that attract people, especially curious, energetic teenagers eager for new experiences. The mainstream, for all its reason and security, is far from perfect. The street offers some real alternatives to the actual and perceived shortcomings of the mainstream. You need to understand that bright side of the street as well as the dark side if you are going to prevent teenagers from going there and bring those who have back to the mainstream alive.

The Lure of the Street

Adolescence, as we know it in the United States today, is a relatively new phenomenon. Prior to the turn of the century, adolescence only lasted long enough for a young man or woman to achieve biological maturity and psychological independence. That normally took two to five years from onset of puberty. Many young men and women in the late 1800s went to work, started their own families, and otherwise took their places as adult members of mainstream society by the time they were fifteen or sixteen years old. Then a couple of things started to happen. First, there was a change in the economic structure of the nation that shifted us from an agrarian to an industrial society. Next, there was an influx of immigrants from central and eastern Europe. This change in the makeup of our population was accompanied by a biological acceleration of puberty. Taken together, these changes created more competition for jobs, which was seen as a threat to the average breadwinner. As a nation, we responded to that threat by extending adolescence and thereby eliminating some of those people from the workforce. We rationalized this decision by telling ourselves that, while young people may be biologically and psychologically ready for adulthood in their mid-teens, they were not sufficiently prepared intellectually or spiritually to function as adults.

We extended adolescence the way we do everything in the mainstream, by passing a law. The law requires young people to attend school until they are sixteen years of age. Then, over a period of time, we structured the public school system such that teenagers can't complete their basic schooling until they are eighteen. We reinforced what we had done by passing additional laws that made it difficult, if not impossible, for anyone under the age of eighteen to get a meaningful job, sign a contract, or otherwise function independently in mainstream society.

Extending adolescence in this way probably seemed like a good idea at the time, and it may have been. However, it has a serious drawback, one that is becoming more and more apparent as we deal with each new generation of teenagers. Since teenagers aren't given an opportunity to support themselves, they have little choice other than to continue to be dependent on their parents who, in turn, continue to treat them as dependents. This dependent relationship is incompatible with the natural development of the biological and psychological self.

The course of biological development is obvious. A young person becomes big enough and strong enough to take care of himself or herself and able to procreate by the age of fourteen or fifteen, sometimes sooner. Biological maturity is accompanied by a powerful urge to try out one's new capabilities. It's Nature's way of preserving one's genes (get people to reproduce before anything happens to them). But mainstream society in this country says to the teenager, "Never mind what Nature says. You can't use your new-found physical prowess until you finish high school." This restriction has about the same effect as giving a son or daughter a Christmas present and telling him or her not to open the present until the Fourth of July.

Psychological independence is a little more difficult to observe. You almost have to listen for it. It begins with Dad telling Junior, "You have to come in now and get cleaned up. We're going to visit Grandma." Junior replies, as he has for years, "I don't want to go to Grandma's. I want to play with my friends." Dad insists, as he has for years, "I don't care. You're going to Grandma's." Suddenly Junior changes the script. He looks Dad straight in the eye and says, "You can't make me."

Or it begins with Sis coming downstairs with green dye in her hair. Mom takes one look and announces, "You're not going out looking like that." Sis replies, as she has for years, "But Mom, why not?" Mom responds as she has for years, "Because I don't approve. That's why not." Then Sis changes the script. She strikes a defiant pose and says, "Well, I'm not you."

What is happening to Junior and Sis happens to all teenagers. It is a process psychologists call differentiation. Like biological maturity, it begins with puberty. Teenagers start to rival their parents in size, logical powers, and competence and begin to feel a biological urge to distance themselves from their parents to start their own families. It intensifies as teenagers realize that they are not extensions of their parents, that they are separate and unique human beings capable of independent thought and action. With that realization comes another powerful urge, the urge to be their own person, which means to form their own ideas and make their own decisions. Psychological independence is another Christmas present that reads, "Don't open until the Fourth of July." The mind says, "I can think for myself," but mainstream society says, "You have to think the way we tell you to until you finish high school."

The process of differentiation is a very powerful one and it will not be denied. Teenagers fight against the restraints being placed on them. Do you remember the "hippie generation"? They had long hair, wore tie-dye clothes, and were committed to social issues. Their children were the "me generation." They had short hair, wore designer clothes, and were committed to themselves. Their kids are the "digital generation." They shave their heads, don't care what they wear and are committed to cyberspace. It's a way of saying to your parents, "I'm not you and you can't make me be you." Every generation of teenagers does it. Every generation of teenagers sets itself apart from its parents. And it's a good thing young people have this instinctive need to strike out on their own. If they didn't we'd probably still be huddled in caves eating roots.

The problem is that the conflict between the need teenagers have to exercise their newfound biological maturity and psychological independence and the restrictions being placed on their doing so by mainstream society can be extremely painful. Most teenagers who have been subjected to this crucible have survived the ordeal, but not necessarily without scars. There are an awful lot of unhappy adults in our society today suffering from debilitating neuroses, phobias, inhibitions, and compulsions that can be traced to their adolescent experiences. Obviously, some teenagers don't survive the ordeal. They commit suicide, run away from home never to be heard from again, or just flip out and wind up in a mental institution. An increasing number of today's teenagers have discovered another option, a way to avoid this crucible. It's an option that has always been available to teenagers. It was available to me. It was available to you, too. Maybe you didn't choose it, or never realized it was there, or never realized that you did choose it for a while. But it was there. That option is the street.

The obvious next question is: Why do some teenagers endure adolescence in the mainstream while others flee to the street? There are probably as many specific answers to that question as there are teenagers. Each set of circumstances is different and each decision is personal. There are, however, some generalities that apply.

First, many of the teenagers on the street today didn't drop out of the mainstream. They were never in the mainstream. They were born and raised in the street society. Their parents were, and probably still are, street people. They were taught from a very early age that life is about survival. They didn't have to reject their parents' beliefs or rebel against their parents' demands to find independence because as soon as they were physically able to take care of themselves, sometimes even before that, they were turned out on their own to fend for themselves. Their problem isn't one of being held back. If anything, they were forced to become adults too soon.

These teenagers don't aspire to the mainstream. As street people, they see the mainstream as their enemy, and rightfully so because, as street people, it is their enemy. They may prey on the mainstream, but they do so in the dark of night, in secluded alleys or with masks on because they are afraid of it. They view the mainstream as a reality they must learn to deal with in order to survive, not as something they want to or could be part of.

Second, there are those teenagers who were born and raised in the mainstream society but lose sight of it or faith in it. They become disillusioned. This happens in one of two ways.

Some teenagers are confused by the apparent contradictions and inconsistencies that exist between what they hear adults say and what they see adults do. There used to be a time when we could shelter teenagers from these kinds of contradictions and inconsistencies. We could tell them whatever we wanted them to hear about what was right and wrong, about who did what to whom, about anything; and we could prevent them from hearing or seeing otherwise. Those were simpler times. Those were also ignorant times and isolation, segregation, and censorship were the tools of ignorance.

Times have changed. Television, the Internet, and the new mobility have seen to that. It is no longer possible to conceal our disagreements or cover up our embarrassing moments the way we once could. Teenagers today are exposed to more information than ever before in history. If they have not been given a valid conceptual framework to operate from and if they have not developed critical thinking skills by the time they reach adolescence, they have no way to reconcile the discrepancies they experience around them. Their confusion often leads to disillusionment. These teenagers lose sight of the fact that there is a line between the two societies. They stop believing the mainstream exists and begin to see the whole country as a survival-based society with some people just doing a better job of surviving than others. They start seeing the whole country as the street.

Do you remember that gray area I talked about earlier that shrouds the line that separates the street from the mainstream? Most teenagers don't know about that gray area. They don't understand that getting around the law is not the same as breaking the law. They don't recognize the fine distinction that exists between being on the line and crossing over it. They may not see the difference between selling people something they don't need and can't really afford, which is a moral issue and doesn't put you over the line, and stealing their money, which is a legal issue and does put you over the line. One of the reasons they may not understand these distinctions is that the standard of behavior we apply to teenagers doesn't have a gray area. The status offenses I talked about earlier essentially say that anything teenagers do that we don't want them to do is illegal and can cost them their freedom. So, by operating in that gray area close to the line yourself, you may be inadvertently contributing to teenagers' confusion and disillusionment and, in a sense, pushing them into the street.

Here is an example.

A middle-class couple is into loopholes. They are always looking for an angle, a way to get an edge, and they talk openly about it. "Not a problem. We can get around this easily." "Your brother-in-law is an idiot. If he had half a brain he could get around that stupid law, like we did, and double his profits." They are good at using loopholes to further their ambitions and they like the challenge. They are bright, well educated, and make enough money to be able to afford good lawyers to guide them. They've never actually crossed the line. Their teenage daughter, however, doesn't understand that using loopholes is acceptable mainstream behavior. It sounds like cheating to her and cheating is, after all, breaking the law. The picture she gets is that her parents cheat and are good at it because they never get caught. More important, they think that people who don't do what they do are "idiots." So, she starts to believe that cheating, or breaking the law, is okay as long as you are smart enough not to get caught. Not only that, she begins to think that if you have the brains and the resources to cheat and get away with it, and she thinks she does, you are an idiot if you don't use them to your advantage. Next thing you know she's forging her father's signature on a note excusing her from school, stealing the answers to the math midterm exam, and selling the diet pills her mother got for her to her friends. The tragedy in this example isn't just that the daughter has crossed the line; the tragedy is that in her mind the line no longer exists.

The other type of disillusionment has to do with self-esteem, or the lack of it. When teenagers don't feel good about themselves they often feel they aren't worthy of the mainstream. They don't lose sight of it. They still know it's out there. They just feel they don't deserve to be part of it. This type of disillusionment is common among teenagers who belong to an ethnic group that has experienced the ego-shattering effects of discrimination and institutional racism. It is also becoming quite common among teenagers from middle-income and well-to-do families, regardless of ethnic background, who have been pushed too hard to meet the expectations of parents, teachers, and friends, and have come up short.

For disillusioned teenagers who have crossed over to the street, the idea of returning to the mainstream doesn't make much sense because, in their minds, the mainstream doesn't really exist—or, if it does, they don't deserve to be part of it.

Need is another reason teenagers go to the street. Teenagers have needs just like everyone else. They need to be somebody. They need to belong someplace. They need to feel loved and safe. They need food, clothing, and shelter. The main difference between teenagers' needs and adults' needs is that teenagers have not had time to develop the coping mechanisms that would enable them to control the powerful emotions like anxiety, disappointment, frustration, anger, and grief that they experience when their needs aren't met. In addition, teenagers' moods tend to shift faster than adults' moods. That's hormonal. They also have a foreshortened sense of time because they haven't been around very long. These factors come together to create a greater sense of urgency for teenagers to meet their needs.

Many teenagers are finding it difficult, if not impossible, to meet their needs in the mainstream. Inner city teenagers, particularly those who come from low income families, get tired of doing without, getting turned away, and being afraid. Their friends tell them they can get what they need on the street—and the truth is they can. Not only can they get what they need on the street, they can get more of it and they can get it faster. So that's where they go.

Middle-class teenagers get tired of being pushed, tired of having to use their time and energy to live up to someone else's expectations. Their friends tell them they don't have to live up to anyone else's expectations on the street— and they don't. They can use their time and energy on the street to concentrate on meeting their own needs. So that's where they go.

You know and I know that teenagers can't keep what they get on the street. We know the street is a dead end. But teenagers don't know that or they choose not to believe it. All they know is the street gives them what the mainstream won't. They have no interest in coming back to the mainstream and won't have any interest in doing so unless and until they find out the street is a dead end and are assured their needs can be met in the mainstream.

Finally, there are those teenagers who wander across the line while testing limits and get trapped on the other side. Testing limits is part of growing up. After all, what good is having a mind of your own and a body that finally works if you can't use them? Testing limits is a way of generating personal experiences against which one can measure one's own strength and on which one can base one's own thoughts and beliefs. So it is not unusual for a mainstream teenager to test the mainstream's laws.

The lucky ones take a few steps across the line and figure out almost immediately that the street is a dead end. They get hurt or scared on the street and decide the potential gains aren't worth the inherent risks. They slip back to the mainstream before anyone even notices they left. They still have the threat of getting caught for the things they did on the street hanging over them, as I explained in the previous chapter, but they are the lucky ones. The unlucky ones stray far enough across the line to become offensive to the mainstream and find the door has been slammed shut behind them. They can't get back to the mainstream without paying a price (their liberty) even if they want to.

The saddest part of this scenario is that it usually isn't the criminal justice system that slams the door on them. It is often the teenagers' own parents or guardians who do the slamming. They label them "ungrateful" or "no good" and disown them by literally locking them out of the house, or by imposing such stifling terms on their continued residence that the teenager has no choice but to leave or suffocate. Schools are also great door slammers. They are quick to label students who have crossed the line and then systematically separate those students from the educational opportunities that might otherwise be available to them through the educational system. Punishment, in all its many forms, is another door slammer. I'll be talking more about punishment later in the book. I'll also be offering some positive alternatives to punishment.

This is by no means intended to be an exhaustive discussion of adolescence or of the reasons teenagers drop out of the mainstream. In fact, our understanding of adolescence is still very limited. What we do know is that each person is unique and each teenager's specific reason for being on the street is different. What I have attempted to do here is provide a general understanding of the problem. I don't expect you to agree with everything I've said. I do think, however, that most teenagers will find it strikes a familiar chord. If you have teenage children, or work with teenagers, I'd like to suggest you ask them to read this chapter and then discuss it with them. The insights that might be gained from such a discussion would far outweigh any light I may have shed on the subject.

What You Can Do

I f there are teenagers in your life that you care about, you obviously don't want them to become part of the teenage dropout problem. You don't want them dropping out of the mainstream because you know they will wind up dead or in jail on the street. You have some idea why they might drop out, but that doesn't necessarily tell you what you can do to prevent them from dropping out or, if they've already dropped out, what you can do to bring them back to the mainstream alive. What you can do to help the teenagers in your life get out and stay out of trouble is what the rest of this book is about.

Let's start with what you can't do. You can't make anybody do anything. If you have enough physical force at your disposal you can keep people from doing something. You can hold them back, tie them down, lock them up, even take their life so they can't do what they want to do. But no amount of physical force can make people do something they choose not to do. That's how the criminal justice system works in this country. It doesn't make anyone behave. It keeps people from misbehaving.

I know this is counterintuitive. Common sense tells you if you put a gun to a man's head and threaten to kill him, he will do whatever you want him to do. Common sense tells you if you threaten a woman's child, she will do anything you tell her to do to protect the child. But experience says that's not true. History is filled with stories of men who were brutally tortured and of women who watched their children die right before their eyes, and still would not do what their persecutors wanted them to do. History is filled with martyrs.

The true nature of power is that it is given, not taken. People who believe that power is taken and held over them are destined to be victims all their lives. Each of us has the power to control our own lives and is free to give it, or not give it, to whomever we want. However, none of us can control the world around us so there are going to be consequences for every choice we make. As long as we are willing to accept the consequences of the choices we make, we control our own lives.

Let's look at a few examples.

When you go to work for an employer you give the employer the power to tell you what to do. The consequence is the employer pays you a salary. You can take that power back anytime you want to. The consequence will be that the employer will no longer pay you a salary if he or she can no longer tell you what to do, and you will have to find another way to make the money you need. The choice is yours. The power is in your hands.

You're at a bar with some friends. A drunk calls you a name. You hit him pretty hard and break his nose. He calls the police and has you arrested for assault. Your excuse is he made you angry. But that's not what happened. What happened is he did something that was offensive to you but not illegal, and you chose to do something illegal to him in response. You gave him power over you. You chose to get angry and retaliate. You didn't have to do that. You could have ignored the remark and walked away. If you had not given him the power he could not have had you arrested. It was your choice. The power was in your hands.

The river floods and destroys your home. You can't control that. But if it is the third time in ten years a flood has destroyed your home, you may want to consider rebuilding on higher ground. You can't control the world around you, but you can control how you react to it. You can give the river power over you and live at its mercy or you can move out of its reach. The consequence of moving may be that you can't afford as big a house on higher ground. So you have to decide between a smaller house that stays dry and a bigger one that gets flooded out whenever the river rises. It's up to you whether you get flooded out every couple of years, not up to the river. The choice is yours. The power is in your hands.

So what does all this have to do with teenagers? It's simple. You can't make them do what you want them to do if they choose not to do it. I know that may be a hard pill to swallow, especially if it is your own child we're talking about. But it is a pill you're going to have to find a way to get down if you want to have an impact on the lives of teenagers. You can lock them in their rooms until they're twenty years old so they can't get in trouble, but that isn't practical and the minute you set them free they'll go right out and do what they wanted to do when you locked them up. So you will not have prevented their getting in trouble, just delayed it.

What you can do is try to influence the choices they make. You can try to help them see that the street is a dead end; and you can try to show them how they can get what they need and want in the mainstream so they will choose to stay in the mainstream, or come back to it if they've already crossed the line.

Obviously your preference is going to be to try to prevent the teenagers in your life from ever crossing over the line to the street in the first place. That can be done. It is very difficult to do, but it can be done. It is actually quite a bit easier to bring teenagers back from the street after they have crossed the line than it is to prevent them from crossing the line in the first place, but prevention is still worth trying. You just need to be realistic about it. You need to understand what you are up against and what you can expect so that you can set reasonable and attainable goals for yourself.

Let's look at each of the basic reasons teenagers go to the street and consider what you might be able to do, and what you might not be able to do, to prevent them from crossing the line.

The teenagers who were born on the street are already there. If you bring them back to the mainstream you will prevent their children from being born on the street, but clearly if someone is already on the street you can't prevent her or him from going there.

You probably can prevent many of the disillusioned teenagers from dropping out of the mainstream if—and it's a big if—you can minimize or eliminate the contradictions and inconsistencies that confuse and disillusion them. That is difficult to do because the things that confuse and disillusion teenagers are not all within your control. Disillusionment is rarely a response to a single experience. Even if you are disciplined enough to ensure that your words and deeds are consistent, there are so many discrepancies, so much misinformation, in the larger mainstream society around you that what you say or do in dealing with teenagers can be, and often is, offset by what others say and do.

The public schools provide an example. They are controlled by local school boards who limit the curriculum to reflect their own preferences and biases. As a result, schools don't really address the complexities of the modern world and are not prepared to explain its many contradictions and inconsistencies in any meaningful or useful way. In fact, the narrow focus of their curricula often creates contradictions and inconsistencies. The objective of many secondary schools in this country is not to provide teenagers the opportunity to discuss and explore ideas, resolve differences, and solve problems. Their objective is to teach students the "right" answers so they can get good grades on standardized tests and move on. Schools could be part of the solution. They could be providing clarification, information, explanation, context, perspective, and models to help teenagers sort things out for themselves (and some educators do that). But more often than not, schools only add to the confusion and eventual disillusionment of their students.

The media, both news and entertainment, don't help, either, although they could if they were objective and analytical and committed to reflecting and representing reality so that people could interpret and understand events in context (and some journalists, writers, filmmakers, etc., do that). But sensationalism is sexier than reality. Fanning the flames of controversy sells better than putting events in perspective. Blowing stuff up is easier than creating stimulating dialog so the media glorify the street, make heroes of criminals, and contribute to the disillusionment.

You can see your job is cut out for you if you want to minimize or eliminate the contradictions and inconsistencies

that disillusion teenagers and drive them to the street. It
gets worse. The street has a distinct advantage when it
comes to disillusionment.

There are far fewer contradictions and inconsistencies
on the street than there are in the mainstream. There is an
inherent directness about the street. Remember that the
gray area we talked about earlier is on the mainstream
side of the line. If you are operating in that gray area you
can look like you are across the line but really not be. It's
sort of built in hypocrisy. For better or worse, it is a part
of mainstream society. It always has been and probably
always will be. There is no such hypocrisy on the street
side of the line. Once you are across the line, you are
across the line. There is no gray area.

The street is also much more intense than the mainstream. A mistake in the mainstream is a setback. A mistake on the street can mean imprisonment or death. There
is less room for subtle intellectual distinctions when your
life is on the line, less interest in gamesmanship when
your liberty is at stake. Teenagers perceive this directness
as being "up front" or honest, and they respect it. The
street may be harsh and violent, but it doesn't lie to them.
In contrast, the mainstream appears to lie to them all the
time. It tells them one thing and then does another.

The most glaring example of this kind of double message is the way the mainstream deals with drugs. It tells
teenagers drugs are bad for them and they shouldn't use
drugs. Then it goes out of its way to convince those same
teenagers that drinking beer and smoking cigarettes are
responsible adult behavior that they should aspire to as
soon as they are of age. Teenagers hate being lied to. They
see it as an insult to their intelligence and a threat to their
emerging independence. Unfortunately, they tend to see
the mainstream as lying to them a lot and the street as

being straight with them, and that makes the street seem attractive in comparison.

Disillusionment with the mainstream is a much easier battle to fight once someone has been on the street a while and experienced the constant terror and inevitable horror that makes it the dead end it is. The inequities of the mainstream don't look quite as bad when compared to the real brutality of the street, but to the disillusioned teenager looking across the fence, the grass on the street side can look greener.

What you can do is openly discuss inconsistencies with teenagers. Help them to understand that to be inconsistent is to be human. Use examples from your own life and from their lives to point out how human beings make mistakes and contradict themselves. Talk about how inconsistency is necessary for growth. Consider what life would be like if one could never change one's mind because that would be inconsistent. And talk about (not tell) what they might be able to legally do to change the inconsistencies that bother and confuse them. Conversations like these can do no harm. They can only help. And if the disillusioned teenagers you talk with wind up on the street anyway, don't despair. You'll get another shot at them after they cross the line.

What about the teenagers who lose, or never had, self-esteem? Can you prevent them from crossing the line? Absolutely. You are still at a disadvantage, but it is one you can overcome. The disadvantage is that the mainstream is a very competitive society. We seem to have adopted Hall of Fame Football Coach Vince Lombardi's philosophy that, "Winning isn't the most important thing, it's the only thing." We've convinced ourselves that if we accept second best, we will never be the best. So, we don't accept second best. That's great for the people who finish first, but it makes everyone else a loser. Nike immortalized that sentiment in a commercial they ran during the Olympic Games in Atlanta. "You don't win the silver," it said, "You lose the gold." Think about the message that sends to our children. It says accomplishment doesn't matter; only winning does. That message doesn't do much for the self-esteem of everyone who doesn't finish first.

And the mainstream doesn't limit this attitude to sports. We lay this winning trip on everybody and it puts incredible pressure on teenagers. Here they are trying to figure out who they are and what they want to do with their lives, and we push this incessant message in their faces that says, "Whatever you do with your life, remember, if you're not number one at it, you're a loser."

Is it really any wonder the street looks attractive in comparison? Winning is not an issue on the street. The street is about surviving, about "getting over." If you don't "get over," you're dead or in jail and it really doesn't matter anymore. You're on your own on the street. You have only yourself to answer to. You don't have to live up to anybody else's expectations. You are free from the pressure of achieving, winning, being the best. There is room on the street for ambition. You can be "top dog" on the street if you are willing to work for it, willing to take the risks and make the sacrifices. But you don't have to be "top dog." No one is expecting that of you. All you have to do is survive. If you can survive, you can feel good about yourself. Can you see how that might be tempting to someone who is always being pushed to be the best?

Fortunately, you can counteract that pressure. The closer you are to a teenager, the better able you are to relieve the pressure because the closer you are the more immediate your feedback is and the more important it becomes. You can tell and show teenagers through your words and actions how much you value and appreciate them. You can encourage and support them, you can praise them, and you can give them reason to feel good about themselves. There are some subtleties to doing this that have to do with respecting the awkwardness of adolescence. For example, praising your son or daughter privately for doing well on a school assignment and encouraging him or her to share the good news with others is preferable to announcing the accomplishment at a family reunion. If you'll just try to remember what you felt like when you were a teenager and try to be sensitive to those feelings in other teenagers you can learn the appropriate subtleties. If you are sincere in your praise, you really can make a significant difference and prevent teenagers from crossing over the line in search of self-esteem.

How do you prevent teenagers from crossing the line to meet their needs? There are no sure answers, no guarantees. However, if you show them how to get high listening to music, or get a rush from white water rafting, or find peace of mind and tranquility in painting or meditating, then they may not feel they have to use drugs to experience those feelings. If you teach teenagers skills that they can use to make money so they can buy the things they need and want, then they may not feel they have to steal those things. If you recognize teenagers as individuals, make them feel appreciated and a part of a family, a school, or a community, then they may not feel they have to join gangs to belong.

It's as simple as it sounds. Show (please note I said show, not tell) teenagers how they can get what they need and want, especially what they need, in the mainstream and they will be far less likely to go looking for it on the street. How do you know what they need? Ask them. Listen to them. They'll tell you. Maybe not straight out. Maybe not directly, but they will tell you. And keep asking. Their needs and wants change.

This is something you're going to have to make time for. You can't do it when it fits into your schedule or when it's convenient. A teenager's personal clock is different from an adult's clock. Adult clocks are compartmentalized. There is now, later, tomorrow, next week, etc. A teenager's clock only has one setting—now. When they want to talk, that's the time to talk. I don't care if you are in the middle of doing something. Put it aside and sit down and talk. You may not get another chance. Your son or daughter may come down to breakfast one Friday morning and say, out of the clear blue, "Remember that day (which may have been six months ago) we were talking about going camping up at the lake. Well, I was thinking, that might not be so bad." If that happens, start packing the car. I don't care if you had plans for the weekend with the Queen of England. Cancel them and go camping with your kid.

If you really and truly can't stop what you are doing, at least take the time to find out what is on the teenager's mind. Ask what she or he wants to talk about. Ask how long he or she thinks the conversation might take. Explain why you feel you shouldn't interrupt what you are doing or change your plans. Teenagers can be quite reasonable. If you are honest and open with them, they'll sit down with you and plan a time and place for the conversation or activity. Just don't make a habit of putting your needs before theirs. Remember, it is their needs that you are trying to help them meet to keep them from going to the street, so it has to be on their terms.

The last group are the teenagers who cross the line to the street as a part of testing limits. I'm afraid there really isn't much you can do about that. Testing limits is part of growing up. You can talk with them in general terms about testing limits and about the risks involved in doing so and you can try to minimize those risks. Some parents have told their teenage children, "I don't approve of drinking, but if you want to try it, do it in the house and not in an alley or in a friend's car where you can get in trouble." I don't know that I would recommend that approach, but there is something to be said for it. It does minimize the risk.

At the very least, you can make sure the door stays open. You can let teenagers know that if they cross the line, if they break the law, they will have to suffer the consequences, but that you will still love them, that there is a way back and a way for them to make things right.

So, prevention is a mixed bag. There are some things you can do that can make a real difference and there are some things worth trying that may or may not work. I don't want to discourage you. I just want you to appreciate how difficult it is to prevent teenagers from dropping out of the mainstream in this day and age. I want you to understand why it is so difficult and recognize the forces in mainstream society that are working against you. That way, if you do try to prevent teenagers from going to the street and fail, you will not take it personally. You will not feel hurt or betrayed and, most important, you will not give up. I don't want you to put all your hopes on prevention and have them dashed if your attempts don't work. To use an analogy, I don't want you to pour all your water on the forest during the spring rainy season and then, when the forest bursts into flames during the dry, hot summer, have to say, "I used up all my water in the spring. There is nothing more I can do." The forest needs water most when it's starting to burn, and teenagers need help most when they're starting to get into trouble.

Think of prevention as the first round in a ten-round fight. If you win in the first round, that's great. If you don't, all isn't lost. There are plenty of rounds left. In fact, as I suggested earlier, the chances of winning are better in the later rounds. Your chances of bringing teenagers back alive from the street are considerably greater than your chances of preventing them from dropping out of the mainstream in the first place. That's because once teenagers are on the street, instead of having the lure of the street working against you, you have the reality of the street working for you.

There is one more problem associated with prevention that I feel I need to mention. There is no sure fire way to know if it's needed or if it's working. After all, your son isn't likely to come up to you one day and say, "Dad, I've been thinking about what I want to do with my life and I think crime is the life for me." Nor is your daughter likely to tell you, "Hey, Mom, me and my friends are going to the mall this afternoon to steal some stuff." Your son and daughter are also not likely to tell you they were thinking about breaking the law but decided not to because of several conversations you've had with them. What they are most likely to do is tell you what they think you want to hear. That makes knowing if prevention is needed and knowing if it has worked very difficult.

It's like the story about the man who is sent to see a psychiatrist in New York City because he keeps clapping his hands over his head. "Why are you clapping your hands over your head?" the psychiatrist asks. "To keep the wild elephants away," answers the man. "But there are no wild elephants around here," the psychiatrist replies. "The nearest wild elephant is six thousand miles away in Africa." "See?" the man says, "It's working."

You can never really know for sure when the teenagers you live with or work with are thinking about crossing the line. A teenager can be well mannered, well dressed, cooperative and cheerful, get good grades, and be responsive to your every request and be totally into drugs, sex, gang-banging, and all kinds of other illegal activity. Acting straight is a great cover, a great way not to get caught. I talked about it earlier. It's the hiding behind respectability scam. Conversely, a teenager can be belligerent, sloppy, recalcitrant, cranky, uninterested in school, and argue with everything you say to him or her and not have the slightest interest in breaking the law or living the street life.

What I suggest you do to ensure you don't miss the boat, so to speak, is assume that if teenagers are willing to break the rules that are set for them in the home, in school, and in the community, they are capable of breaking the mainstream's laws. Assume that if teenagers are willing to behave without regard for other people's feelings, rights, and safety, they are capable of doing whatever they have to do to get what they need and want, without regard for the harm they may cause other people. Don't expect them to always act like adults. They are not adults yet. But don't dismiss their inappropriate behavior with a casual, "Oh, they'll grow out of it." If they cross the line they may not get the chance to grow out of it. Confront their inappropriate behavior and deal with it because once they are across the line, prevention is no longer an option and intervention becomes necessary.

So, what can you do? You can set standards and expectations for teenagers by being a role model for them. You can openly and honestly discuss the contradictions and inconsistencies that confuse and disillusion them. You can provide them with viable alternatives to the street, alternatives that offer them real opportunity to get what they need and want in mainstream society. You can encourage them to be the special and unique individuals they are and you can give them choices and allow them to accept responsibility for the decisions they make. You can accept them as members of your families, as friends, as students, as citizens, and as the future of our country no matter what they decide. If all that fails and they continue to behave in a negative and inappropriate manner, accept that they may well have crossed the line from the mainstream to the street and help them get back to the mainstream before they wind up dead or in jail.

There is a way to do that, a way to influence the choices teenagers who have crossed the line make so they will choose to come back to the mainstream—a way that works. I call it the Streetwise Strategy. All of the people I told you about earlier who are making a difference in the lives of troubled and troublesome teenagers use some version of this strategy. They may not use it exactly as I am going to describe it to you. They may use different terms to describe what they do, but they all follow some version of these three basic steps:

1. Establish a nonthreatening relationship with the teenagers you are trying to help.
2. Impose the consequences of their behavior.
3. Identify the talents and abilities they are using to survive on the street and redirect those talents and abilities so they can use them to get what they need and want in the mainstream.

The Streetwise Strategy is simple in concept, but not easy to use. It takes a lot of self-discipline and practice to master. You have to work at it to make it work for you, but it can work for you. In actual practice, the steps often overlap and interact. However, since their effect is cumulative and one step must be accomplished before the next step can be effective, it makes sense to examine them one at a time.

Establishing a Nonthreatening Relationship

5

As I've said several times, you can't make teenagers do anything. Whether it's bringing them back from the street or keeping them from going there in the first place, you can only hope to influence the choices they make. To be precise, what you actually influence is a teenager's decision to behave or not behave in a particular way. However, since the behavior is what you see, the end product so to speak, I'm going to talk in terms of influencing behavior, with the understanding that you influence behavior by influencing teenagers' decisions, which determine the choices they make.

The chances of your influencing the behavior of teenagers will not be very good if they perceive you as a threat. This principle applies to all teenagers, but is especially true of teenagers who are on the street because they view enforcers of the law and, by association, all authority figures as their mortal enemies.

Establishing a nonthreatening relationship doesn't mean being permissive or being a buddy to a teenager. It means positioning yourself so as to be perceived as someone who cares about the teenager and is trying to help. You can learn the part about trying to help, but you can't fake caring. If you don't really care about a teenager you are dealing with, he or she will sense it and will be suspicious of both your advice and your motives for giving that advice.

That makes caring a good place to start in establishing a nonthreatening relationship with a teenager. Ask yourself, "Whose interest am I really trying to serve? Am I trying to influence this teenager's behavior because it serves my needs or because it will best serve the teenager's needs?" If your motives are self-serving you can't expect teenagers to buy into them. The biological and psychological stresses of adolescence require that teenagers concentrate their energies on their own development. The intensity of the street demands that they look out for their own needs. Either way, they are not going to pay attention to you if they sense you are not interested in helping them meet their needs.

Remember Sis with the green dye in her hair? If she were your daughter and you were telling her she couldn't go out with green hair, what would your motives be? If she were going on a job interview, you might well be trying to help her get the job she wants. But if she were going to the mall with her girlfriends, whose interest would you be serving? Would you really be afraid that she would do herself some harm by having green dye in her hair, or would you be concerned the neighbors might see her and think less of you as a parent?

Suppose your son loves basketball and is very good at it. He spends more time playing basketball than studying. If you tell your son he should pay more attention to his schoolwork and forget about basketball, whose needs are you serving?

Let's assume your son knows several things:

1. He wants to go to college and you can't afford to send him.
2. He is only an average student and will not get an academic scholarship no matter how hard he studies.
3. He is a very talented basketball player and could get a full scholarship to a good university if he works hard at his basketball.

How are you helping him meet his needs when you discourage his interest in basketball? Or are you just unwilling to accept the fact that your son is not as bright a student as you would like him to be and see that as a reflection on your intelligence?

The worst part about being perceived by teenagers as not caring is that the perception carries over to other issues. If your daughter and son are suspicious of your motives and mistrust your advice on hair color or basketball, they are going to be suspicious of your motives and mistrust your advice when you tell them not to drink and drive, use drugs, have sex, or engage in other behavior where you know their safety and health are truly at risk.

You have to do some soul searching if you want to be able to influence teenage behavior. You have to be willing to help them get what they need and want, not just what you think they should need and want. That's what caring is all about.

As I said earlier, timing is an important part of demonstrating that you care. Teenagers need your attention and assistance when they need it, not just when it's convenient for you to give it. To begin with, they don't have a very good sense of time. Everything seems to be a crisis or an emergency to teenagers. They haven't learned about patience, or priorities, or how to be considerate of other people's needs yet. This constant state of urgency provides a real opportunity for you to show teenagers you care and teach them how to care about other people at the same time. You do that in the following ways:

1. By responding to their needs when they express those needs. You don't necessarily have to resolve a problem or talk a subject completely through at that moment. But you do have to make it clear to teenagers that you are willing to listen and you have to assure them that their needs can be met.

2. By being patient with them. Don't rush them. Don't be in a hurry to "get on with it" or to get back to your own business. Show them there is time by having time.

3. By helping them establish priorities. Break big problems down into smaller, more manageable pieces. Separate complex subjects into simpler topics. Involve them in working out a plan and a schedule to deal with each piece or topic one at a time.

4. By making them aware of your needs. Don't be afraid to tell teenagers about your needs. Put them on the table and consider them along with the teenagers' needs. You might even encourage them to help you meet your needs just as you are helping them meet theirs.

Once you care, and you show teenagers that you care, everything is possible. Assuming you care, there are some specific skills you can use to establish a nonthreatening relationship with teenagers. They are summarized by the word ARC, as in an electric arc that bridges the gap between two opposite poles. ARC stands for Accountability, Respect, and Consistency.

Accountability

Accountability is about letting teenagers know what you expect of them and providing them with feedback on how well they are meeting those expectations. Teenagers don't read minds. You have to tell them what you expect of them. In any given situation, you have to make clear what behavior you consider appropriate and acceptable and what behavior you consider inappropriate or unacceptable. You also have to explain to teenagers why your expectations are important and what the consequences of not meeting those expectations might be. Part of providing an explanation involves establishing a relevant context for the behavior. "Because I said so and I'll tan your hide if you don't," is not an explanation. "Because you want people to trust you and they won't if you lie to them," is an explanation that establishes a relevant context. Once you've established the expectations, then you have to give teenagers feedback. You have to congratulate them when they meet your expectations and you have to confront them when they don't.

Are you surprised? I'm talking about establishing a nonthreatening relationship with teenagers and I'm telling you to confront them when they misbehave. Isn't that contradictory? Not at all. Not to confront unacceptable or inappropriate behavior is to condone it, and to condone behavior that can ultimately be harmful to a teenager is to say to that teenager, "I don't care what you do or what happens to you." People who do not hold teenagers accountable for their behavior are perceived by teenagers as people who don't care about them . . . and if you don't care, you have no influence.

How you confront inappropriate behavior does matter. I am not talking about passing judgment on a teenager for behaving unacceptably or inappropriately. I am talking about putting behavior in context, the context of the street and the mainstream. I am talking about pointing out that there are consequences associated with behaving in a way that is unacceptable to the mainstream. I am talking about being critical of the behavior, not of the person exhibiting that behavior.

Here are some examples.

Suppose you are a high-school teacher. A female student steals $5 from your purse and you find out about it. To say nothing would be to condone the behavior, and you certainly don't want to do that. So you might say, "I'm ashamed of you. You are nothing but a common thief." That's a judgmental statement. What the student hears is, "You don't like me because I took your money."

A better response would be to say, "Taking something that doesn't belong to you is unacceptable behavior. It's stealing, and not only do you hurt the person you steal from, you hurt yourself because you can go to jail for stealing. If you need money that badly, let me know and I'll try to find a way to help you get it." This confrontation is objective. It puts the behavior in context and explains the consequences of that behavior. It is also corrective in that it offers the student an acceptable alternative for meeting her needs in the future.

A student is on lunch break. He is outside the school blasting his tape player. You, the teacher, still have students in class and the noise is distracting them. Given what I have said about accountability, which of the following responses do you think would be most effective?

A. You tell the class to ignore the noise and say nothing to the student with the tape player.
B. You yell out the window at the student with the tape player, "Hey! How about a little consideration? Turn that thing down or I'll take it away from you."
C. You walk outside and say to the student with the tape player, "Excuse me. Your music is really loud. It's disturbing the students who are still in class. Would you please turn it down a little or put on headphones so the students who are still in class can concentrate on their work?"

The answer, of course, is C. The first answer, A, tells the student with the tape player and the students in class you don't care about any of them. B is threatening and will probably elicit a defensive response or no response at all. C will probably get the music turned down and will increase your influence, not only with the student with the radio, but with all the other students in your class as well. Part of the reason C works has to do with the manner in which the student was confronted. The confrontation was respectful and gave the student a way to comply with the request without losing face.

Now suppose the student with the tape player turns his music back up as soon as you walk away? Then you simply reinforce your original message by making it more specific. "Look, I can't allow you to continue to disturb the other students. I've given you some alternatives. Do you want to get in trouble? Do you want someone to take your tape player away from you? Because that is what will happen if you continue to disturb the other students. Why not just turn the music down or put on some headphones? That way you get to listen to your music and the students in class can do their work and everybody is happy."

If you teach in a public school, I can imagine you must be thinking, "I don't have time to do all that. Even if I did, I can't leave my classroom." I understand that. Unfortunately, if you don't do what works you aren't going to get the results you want. If the system you operate under doesn't allow you to do what works, then you are eventually going to have to change that system. Short of changing the system, there are some options available to you. You could call someone to cover your class for a few minutes while you go to talk to the student with the radio. You could ask someone else to talk to the student with the radio. You could even send one of the students from your class to talk to the student with the radio, or ask him to come to your class to talk to you. None of these options is perfect, but they are all a lot better than doing nothing or shouting out the window.

Both of these examples meet all the requirements of accountability. They make clear what is expected; they explain why the expectations are important; they describe the consequences of not meeting the expectations; and they let the students in the examples know that their behavior does not meet those expectations. The teachers in these examples also do something else, something very important. They provide their students with alternatives. The teachers explain to their students how the students can meet their needs in acceptable, appropriate ways. Giving teenagers alternatives when you confront their inappropriate behavior reinforces the message that you care about them and gives them some idea of how they might meet your expectations in the future.

I realize holding teenagers accountable for their behavior is not always going to be easy to do. My point is this: It is essential that you do it if you hope to establish a non-threatening relationship with teenagers, and that means you are going to have to find a way and make the time to do it. You are going to have to make it a priority.

Respect

In every society where there are laws that govern people's behavior, there is also a convention, or norm, which proscribes a manner of interacting with one another that makes it easier to live within those laws. It's called vested, or ascribed, status. We attribute status to certain positions and afford the people who hold those positions a certain degree of respect simply because they hold the position. Parents, teachers, bosses, elders, and certain elected officials fall into this category. We teach that convention to our children and expect them to honor it. "I don't care what Aunt Tillie said to you, she's your Aunt and you have to show her respect." I'm sure you've all heard the line, or one just like it.

The problem is that the concept of vested status doesn't exist in the street society. Consequently, a teenager on the street doesn't recognize vested status and will not respond to it with any measure of respect. The only kind of status that exists on the street is the kind you earn. Respect on the street is based on what you do, not on who you are.

Don't confuse respect with fear. People will treat you any way you want them to if they are afraid of you, but only to your face. As soon as your back is turned, all bets are off. That's not respect. You may be able to frighten some teenagers into behaving a certain way in your presence, but what influence will that have when you're not around? None.

The only way to get teenagers who are living in the street society to treat you with respect is to earn that respect, and the best way to earn it is by giving it—by treating them with respect. Treating teenagers with respect starts with common courtesy. The old, "Do as I say, not as I do," cliché doesn't hold any water. If you want polite, you have to be polite. If you want considerate, you have to be considerate. Even then it isn't a sure thing, but you don't have a leg to stand on if you don't hold yourself to the same standard of behavior you expect from teenagers. Do you let your teenage children barge into your bedroom and flop down on your bed? If you do, then you can barge into their bedroom and flop down on their bed. If, on the other hand, you require them to knock before entering your bedroom and ask permission to sit on your bed, then that's what you have to do when you go to their room.

I know some of you are saying, "Hey, wait a minute. I'm still the parent. As long as I pay the bills, I'll make the rules in my house. That's how my parents raised me and I turned out all right." And you are right. You are the parent and you should set the expectations for behavior in your house, not just because you can, but also because it is your responsibility as a parent to do so. I am not questioning your authority as a parent. I am saying that your teenage children will challenge you and how you respond to that challenge will determine how much influence you have on the decisions they make. You can demand respect if you want to. I'm suggesting you won't get respect that way. I'm suggesting you have to earn your children's respect and you earn their respect by treating them with respect.

I don't mean to be cruel, but the fact that you or I survived adolescence doesn't guarantee that our children will. As parents we want to do everything we can to improve our children's chances of getting through the ordeal of adolescence alive and intact. Earning their respect is one of the ways you establish a nonthreatening relationship with them, and that is essential if you hope to influence their decisions and behavior.

Earning a teenager's respect isn't just something parents need to do. Everyone who deals with teenagers needs to do it.

Let's say you own a clothing store in the local mall. Teenagers are potential customers. They can also be a nuisance when they congregate in front of your store. How would you ask them to move? How would you ask a group of businessmen dressed in suits and ties to move? Would you say, "Go on, get outta here. If I see you punks around here again, I'll call the cops." Or would you say, "Excuse me gentlemen, you may not have noticed, but you're blocking the door to my store. Would you mind moving your conversation down a little bit so my customers can get in and out?"

The first approach is obviously disrespectful. It is an order you have no real authority to give; it assumes these teenagers you don't even know are "punks"; and it is threatening. The second approach assumes the teenagers' good intentions (that they wouldn't deliberately block the door) and puts your request in context.

When it comes to respect, what's good for the goose is good for the gander. If you want a group of teenage boys to act like gentlemen, you have to treat them like gentlemen. If they still act like "punks," you hold them accountable. "Say fellas, I'm speaking to you as adults. I'm treating you with respect. I think I'm making a reasonable request. I'm just asking you to move your conversation down a bit. I'm not telling you to vanish from the face of the earth. If you want me to treat you like a bunch of hoodlums and call the cops and have them roust you, I can do that. But I don't think that's what you want and it's certainly not what I want. Why don't you just move your conversation over by the fountain? That way you can have your conversation, I can run my business, and there won't be any trouble. What do you say?"

Not only will this approach get the teenagers to move, it may bring them back as customers. And it may achieve an additional benefit; it may prompt them to tell their friends not to "mess" with you, maybe even not to "rip you off" because "you're okay." That's the ultimate compliment teenagers can pay you. It means you treat them with respect.

If you deal with teenagers on a regular basis, here are some rules of thumb you can use to earn their respect.

1. Every time you make eye contact with a teenager, acknowledge that teenager. A smile, a "Hi," a "Good morning," a "That's a neat T-shirt," are perceived as signs of respect by teenagers. You acknowledged their existence as human beings at a time when you didn't have to. That will earn you a measure of their respect.

2. Conversely, never look away without first acknowledging a teenager once you've made eye contact with him or her. Teenagers will perceive your looking away without a comment as a sign that you are afraid of them or uncomfortable dealing with them. Don't expect them to initiate social contact. They

usually wait for the adult to do that since they are often treated with disdain by adults.

3. Make it your business to learn teenagers' names and call them by their names whenever you can. It is a sign you recognize them as individuals. That's a sign of respect that will be returned in kind.

4. Always walk over to teenagers before talking to them, especially if you are going to confront and correct their behavior. If it isn't worth walking over to them to say what you have to say, you might as well save your breath. Yelling out the window or down the hall at teenagers will be perceived by them as disrespectful and, consequently, anything you say from that distance will be challenged or disregarded.

5. Always make positive contact with teenagers before confronting and correcting their behavior. Start your speech with a friendly, "Excuse me," or, "How are you today?" This puts you in a positive frame of mind and sets the tone for the ensuing dialog. If your opening is respectful and non-threatening, you can expect the conversation to be civil and rational. If you walk up with an angry or impatient look on your face and verbally jump on teenagers, you're asking for a fight.

This may all sound pretty basic to many of you. After all, it's just common sense. You treat people the way you would want to be treated yourself. It may be common sense, but it sure isn't common practice. Try watching adults deal with teenagers sometime. Find a little corner someplace where you can sit back, listen, and observe. I think you'll be amazed by the lack of respect adults show teenagers. I don't think they are even aware of what they are doing most of the time. Maybe that's because teenagers have no status in the mainstream. They are viewed and treated as nonpersons. The multitude of planned activities (Little League, dance lessons, Boy Scouts, etc.) dry up at about age fourteen for all but the most talented. Except for school, there is no place designed for teenagers to go and very little planned for them to do that is of any interest to them. The soda fountain served this purpose when I was a teenager; more recently, a number of communities have established teen centers, which are run by teens in an effort to meet this need. But, generally speaking, as I said earlier, adults don't seem to want teenagers around, don't have time for teenagers, and don't want to deal with teenagers. Admittedly, teenagers can be difficult to deal with, but the street doesn't mind having them around. That's one of the reasons so many of them are going to the street, and when they get to the street they become even more difficult for adults to deal with. If common courtesy is a matter of common sense, let's start using some common sense.

There is another dimension to respect that needs to be considered in establishing a nonthreatening relationship with teenagers. It has to do with recognizing their individuality and their right to act with a degree of independence. They have to be permitted to make their own decisions and experience the consequences of those decisions. You can try to influence those decisions. You can give advice, share your opinions, explain the risks, describe the options, but ultimately, you have to respect their right to decide for themselves and you have to trust their judgment, their intelligence, and their ability to learn from their mistakes.

I know it is very difficult to let go, especially if the teenager is your child and the risks involved are great, but sometimes you just have to let go in order to hold on. It's like stopping a runaway horse. The more you pull, the more the horse pulls against you and the faster it goes. When you stop pulling, it has nothing to pull against so it slows down. Teenagers are the same way. The more you try to control them, the more they pull away, and the less they listen to what you have to say. When you let go and let them make their own decisions, they stop pulling and may start listening to your advice. It's one of those reverse reaction phenomena that doesn't sound like it would work but does. All I can say is try it. When you begin to see it works you will start to believe in it and find it easier to do.

Here is a fairly typical situation that lends itself to demonstrating this kind of respect. You don't approve of the young man your daughter wants to date. The conversation might go something like this:

YOU: Eileen, I want to talk to you about Bobby. I have some concerns about your going out with him.

EILEEN: Mom, it's none of your business.

YOU: He's not my business, but you are. I'm not saying you can't go out with him. I just want to let you know what my concerns are.

EILEEN: Why don't you like him?

YOU: I didn't say I didn't like him. My friend Sarah, who works at the diner on Main Street, has apparently seen him there several times and she says he drinks. I'm afraid he's going to drink while he's out with you, drive around drunk, and get in an accident.

EILEEN: Mom, don't worry about it. If I tell him not to drink, he won't drink.

YOU: How can you be so sure? You've never been out with him before. Have you?

EILEEN: No, I haven't. But I know him. He'll listen to me.

YOU: What happens if he doesn't? You don't have your license yet.

EILEEN: Mom, he'll listen.

YOU: Can I make a suggestion?

EILEEN: What?

YOU: Could you double date? Just for this first date. That way if he does drink someone else can drive.

EILEEN: I don't know. Maybe.

YOU: Well, think about it. But I want you to promise me one thing. Promise me you'll take money with you and you'll call us to come and pick you up if he's drinking. Will you promise me that?

EILEEN: Okay.

The alternative to this scenario, and a tragically common one, is to forbid Eileen to go out with Bobby. She goes out with him anyway. It's easy enough to fool you. She goes out with her girlfriend Mary and she meets Bobby somewhere later on. It turns out she was wrong about Bobby. He gets drunk and she doesn't want to ride with him. She can't call you to pick her up because you told her not to go out with him and she'll get in trouble if she calls you. So she goes ahead and rides with him and they get in an accident. You have to trust that, given the choices and the options you gave her, Eileen will make the responsible decision.

Here's another example.

You work at a community center and an older teenager, Carlos, is harassing a group of younger teenagers, Marcus, and his friends. The first thing you want to try to do is separate Carlos from the crowd. If he doesn't have an audience he's less likely to put on a performance or "show off." So, you might start by saying, "Excuse me, young man, may I talk to you for a moment? Over here by the water fountain." Let's assume for the purpose of this example that Carlos is belligerent and refuses to step to the side with you. That makes the situation potentially more volatile, but not impossible.

YOU: Well, what seems to be the problem then?

CARLOS: There's no problem, bro.

MARCUS: We're trying to play basketball and he keeps getting in the way and taking the ball.

YOU: So what's that all about?

CARLOS: Hey, bro, I said there's no problem. (*To Marcus*) You shut up. (*Marcus fades back*)

YOU: I don't think I know you. My name is Joe D. I'm a Rec Aide here. What's your name?

CARLOS: What difference does it make?

YOU: It doesn't make any difference. When I talk with somebody I just like to call him or her by their name, that's all.

CARLOS: Why don't you just get out of my face?

YOU: I'll be happy to leave you alone if you'll stay out of the way and let these guys have their game.

CARLOS (*moving closer*): I'm really starting to get pissed off. If you don't get out of my face, I'm gonna hurt you bad.

YOU (*Remaining calm*): I'm sure you could if that's really what you want to do, but then you'd wind up in jail and I don't think that's what you want.

CARLOS: Hey, bro. I don't care about jail.

YOU: Well, it's your decision. I'm not looking for a fight. I'm just asking you to leave these guys alone. If you'd like to join one of our programs here, I'll be happy to help you. If you just want to hang out, that's okay, too, as long as you don't bother other people. That's fair, isn't it? What do you say?

CARLOS (*Walking away*): Yeah, well I'll think about it.

The alternative to this scenario, also a tragically common one, is that you tell Carlos to get out of the center. When he says no and threatens you, you threaten him back. The argument gets louder and draws a crowd. The crowd's attention makes it harder for you or Carlos to back down. The tension escalates, the situation gets out of hand, and eventually the police have to be called to restore order. Again, you have to trust that, given the choices and options you have given Carlos, he will make the responsible decision. You have to let go to hold on. You have to give respect in order to get it.

One thing you should know about street people that is relevant to this scenario is that street people don't play by John Wayne rules. Remember, they have no rules. If they want to hurt you, they hurt you. They don't give you a warning. They don't threaten you. They don't say, "Let's step outside and settle this man to man," not if they really want to hurt you. They come right after you, usually when you're not looking. When street people threaten you they are trying to frighten you, to intimidate you, to back you off. If they can do that, they don't have to get into an actual fight with you and risk getting hurt themselves. If they are threatening you, you are not in immediate danger. You don't want to antagonize them or back them into a corner. However, if you don't get scared and if you give them an alternative that will allow them to back out of the confrontation while still saving face, you won't get hurt. That's what happened with Carlos in the example. It doesn't matter what they are saying. As long as they are talking, there is time for you to talk. You don't have to get hostile or physical in order to protect yourself. You are not in danger. You don't have to protect your image by demonstrating how tough you are. Your image is not at issue. Besides, diffusing a potentially volatile situation will not be perceived as a sign of weakness by teenagers. It will be perceived as a sign of great strength. Meeting a threat with a threat only serves to escalate the confrontation and makes the situation more dangerous than it is. It also serves to validate the use of force as a means of getting what you want. In that sense, it actually reinforces the very behavior you are trying to change. And, of course, it establishes, almost irrevocably, that you are out to hurt teenagers and, therefore, not to be trusted by them.

Consistency

Consistency, as it relates to establishing a nonthreatening relationship with teenagers, means always holding teenagers accountable for their behavior and always treating them with respect. It also means that if several people are dealing with the same teenager, such as a mother and father or the teachers in a school, they all have to hold the teenager accountable and treat him or her with respect all the time. It does not mean always doling out the same punishment for the same infraction of the rules. The Streetwise Strategy is not concerned with retribution. It is about changing behavior, and punishment, as we will discuss in the next chapter, doesn't change behavior. If anything, it reinforces it.

The reason consistency is such an important part of establishing a nonthreatening relationship with teenagers on the street is that inconsistency is one of the principal danger signs on the street. Street people, teenagers included, look for inconsistency in other people's statements and behavior. When they find it, they interpret it as a signal that something is not right, that someone is not being "straight." Their response to this kind of signal is to immediately go on the defensive. You can't reason with them, discuss alternatives with them, or expect them to be truthful with you when they are in a defensive mode.

We're much more tolerant of inconsistency in the mainstream. That's probably because the risks associated with misjudging someone's statements or actions are not so great. We go to buy a used car. The car is ten years old, but the odometer only reads 20,000 miles. We notice the inconsistency. We ask about the discrepancy. But we dismiss our concern when the salesman tells us the car was driven by a "little old lady." We know there is such a thing as a bargain and we choose to believe we have found one. We may think about asking for proof, but if we find the salesman to be likeable we probably take his word for it. After all, if it turns out we are wrong and the car really has 80,000 miles on it, the worst that happens is we have to make some repairs to it and we are out some additional money. Besides, we have some recourse through the Better Business Bureau and we can always sue in civil court if we feel we have been intentionally cheated.

That's not the way it works on the street. You're turning tricks in a bar and you meet a guy who says he's in town for the week on business. Later in the conversation he mentions he likes the house band at one of the local night spots. How does he know about the night spot and the house band if he's from out of town? There's an inconsistency here, and you'd better get it cleared up before you offer to perform sexual favors for money. Why is he lying about being from out of town? What is he hiding? Is he a cop? Make a mistake, offer to perform sexual favors and it turns out he is a cop, and you wind up in jail. No, inconsistencies can't be overlooked. Not on the street. And because of that, street people become very sensitive to inconsistencies. They can spot them in an instant and will go on the defensive when they do.

Another thing you need to understand about the street relative to consistency (or the lack of it) is that street people place a much higher value on nonverbal communication than we do in the mainstream. Mainstream society in the United States has a linear orientation. We place greater emphasis on language as a means of communication than we do on other forms of communication. Our motto is, "Do as I say, not as I do." We revere the spoken and written word. We appear to be easily swayed by an advertiser's claims and a politician's promises, even to the point of overlooking our own experience with a product or a politician's voting record. Research shows we tend to place more value on the recommendation of a neighbor than on statistical evidence.

For street people, actions speak louder than words. Hence the street expressions, "Talk is cheap," "Put up or shut up," and "What are you gonna do about it?" On the street, what you do is more important than what you say. Consequently, in dealing with teenagers on the street your actions must be consistent with your statements if you want to have a positive influence on their behavior. You can't tell your daughter that stealing is unacceptable behavior after she has seen you switch the price tag on a dress you bought in a department store. You can't tell your son that hitting other people is unacceptable behavior after he sees you threaten to kick the neighbor's butt if his dog gets in your yard again. You can't tell teenagers you care about them and then not have time for them when they need your attention or assistance. You can't tell teenagers you respect their intelligence and then not let them make their own decisions. In each of these cases your nonverbal message contradicts your verbal message. That's inconsistent and will put teenagers off.

It is not reasonable or realistic to expect perfection. No matter how hard you try to be consistent, the time will come when you just plain blow it. You'll be preoccupied, or aggravated, or just have a bad day and you'll be inconsistent in your dealings with a teenager. It's not the end of the world, or more specifically, it's not the end of your nonthreatening relationship, provided you apologize. That's right, apologize. Call the teenager aside when your composure has returned and say, "You know, I really don't appreciate your using foul language in my presence, but that doesn't excuse my yelling at you the way I did yesterday. I know you were angry because I didn't take the time to listen to you. I really was very busy, but looking back, I guess I should have made the time. I'm sorry it turned out the way it did." You'll probably get, "It's okay. I'm sorry I cursed at you," as a reply, to which you might respond, "Well, maybe we can both try to do better next time."

Making a mistake doesn't mean you are inconsistent. Making an incorrect assumption, an unfair decision, or reacting inappropriately just means you are human. Don't be afraid to own up to your mistakes. Admit you made an error or acted unreasonably. It will not only restore a nonthreatening relationship with a teenager, it will serve as a valuable lesson for the teenager, especially one from the street. There are no apologies on the street. They are a sign of weakness and will get you hurt. Showing teenagers that change is possible, that mistakes need not be permanent, that they can make things right, is showing them there is a way back from the street.

Consistency also means you keep trying. Many people will try using a nonthreatening approach once or twice. Then, if they don't get a positive response right away, they revert back to the "hard line." You have to continue to hold teenagers accountable for their behavior for as long as they continue to behave inappropriately. You have to continue to show teenagers respect even if they don't show you respect. You have to set the tone. You have to be the role model. You have to continue to be nonthreatening. Remember, too, that teenagers will hear you if you are nonthreatening even before they begin to respond to you.

There is one more point I want to make on the subject of establishing a nonthreatening relationship. It's a subtle point but an important one. You may have noticed it in some of the examples I used earlier. Whenever you make reference to punishment, speak of it in the third person. Don't position yourself as the initiator of punishment. Say, "You can go to jail for this," not, "I'll have you arrested." Say, "If you keep that up you are going to get yourself in a lot of trouble," not, "If you don't stop that right now I'll call the cops."

There are two reasons for referring to punishment in the third person. First, it confirms that you are not a threat. It is obvious to a teenager that you are in a position to have them arrested, or initiate punitive action. By not positioning yourself as the initiator, however, you are saying to a teenager, "I don't want to hurt you. I want to help you," and that, after all, is the basis of a nonthreatening relationship.

Second, it sets the stage for imposing the consequences of street behavior, which is the next step in the Streetwise Strategy. It points out the risks of breaking the law, but it does so by placing responsibility for the outcome in the teenager's own hands. It gives the teenager a choice, an option to consider. It suggests, "This could happen to you, but it doesn't have to. You can choose. There is a way to get what you need and want that doesn't have the same risks. There is a way to get what you need and want in the mainstream and a way to get back to the mainstream alive."

6

Imposing Consequences

Two things have to happen before teenagers who have chosen to live in the street society will even consider coming back to the mainstream. First, they must come to seriously doubt, not just in their heads but also in their hearts, that they can continue to survive on the street. Second, they need to be convinced that the mainstream is real and they can get what they need and want there. Imposing the consequences of their street behavior is how you get teenagers to doubt their ability to continue surviving on the street. It also lays the groundwork for convincing them the mainstream is real and showing them how they can get what they need and want there.

Imposing the consequences of street behavior is more than just holding teenagers accountable for their behavior. Holding teenagers accountable, as I said earlier, is about expectations and feedback. It involves telling teenagers what you expect of them and why it matters, letting them know whether or not they are meeting those expectation, describing the consequences of meeting or not meeting the expectations, and suggesting alternative behaviors that might help them meet the expectations in the future. It is an essential part of establishing a non-threatening relationship with teenagers because it shows them you care, but it doesn't go far enough.

Talk is cheap, especially on the street. So, even if teenagers understand the possible consequences of their behavior on an intellectual level, many of them will continue to believe that they can avoid those consequences. Imposing the consequences of street behavior goes beyond holding teenagers accountable for their behavior. It requires that teenagers actually experience the consequences of their street behavior, not just hear about those consequences.

This is going to be very difficult to do because the consequences of street behavior can be emotionally and physically painful for teenagers. It is going to be hard for you to watch teenagers you care about suffer these consequences. It will be even harder to be the person who brings these consequences to bear. However, if you don't do it, not only don't you become part of the solution, you become part of the problem. By actively or tacitly helping teenagers avoid experiencing the consequences of street behavior you enable them to continue surviving on the street. And as long as they can survive on the street, there is no reason for them to come back to the mainstream. Remember, whatever you can get in the mainstream, you can get more of it and get it faster on the street. There is no confusing gray area on the street that looks like one thing but is really something else. The street places no expectations on you and you can get as much respect as you can earn. Plus, the street is exciting. As one of my students so aptly described the attraction, "Why would I want to work for someone else forty hours a week for $200 when I can make $200 an hour rollin' dope (selling drugs) whenever I feel like it?" Fortunately, this young lady learned that, "Money don't love you back, like you love it." She discovered the street was a dead end and made it back to the mainstream.

There are two types of consequences that result from street behavior—direct consequences and indirect consequences.

When teenagers break the law, they harm other people. The harm they cause is the direct consequence, or result, of their street behavior. In order to experience that direct consequence, teenagers must undo the harm they've done.

The indirect consequences of street behavior are what other people may choose to do in response to someone's breaking the law. Being punished for breaking the law is an indirect consequence of the behavior because someone else has to choose to do it. For example, if you punch me in the face and break my nose, I am going to hurt and will have to go to the hospital to have my nose fixed. That's the direct consequence of your behavior. If I choose to punish you for breaking my nose by calling the police and having you arrested for assault, that would be an indirect consequence of your behavior. What makes that consequence indirect is that I have to choose to have you arrested. I could also choose not to punish you, to do nothing, and there would be no indirect consequence of your punching me. But there would still be a direct, inevitable consequence—my broken nose. The fact that someone else has to choose to respond to the behavior makes indirect consequences, and punishment, somewhat arbitrary.

The mainstream in the United States has chosen to punish those who break its laws by depriving the guilty party of his or her freedom to participate in the mainstream by isolating him or her from the mainstream. There are other ways societies punish lawbreakers. Retaliation in the form of inflicting pain is one way; and some societies do, in fact, cane offenders. Retribution, as in "an eye for an eye," is another form of punishment still used by some societies. Steal something and we cut off your hand. We don't do those things in the mainstream in the United States. We isolate the people who break our laws. In a society that operates without regard for laws, like the street, I could do anything I wanted to do to punish you for hurting me. I could steal your car, rape your girlfriend, or have my friend, Big Ernie, break your nose.

The logic of our chosen form of punishment in the mainstream is simple and makes sense. We believe retaliation and retribution are cruel and inhumane. We also believe that if we make a law against a certain behavior, it is because we consider the behavior to be a threat to our safety and security and the best way to prevent someone who has broken the law from breaking it again is to remove the offending individual from our society. This principle of punishment applies in all jurisdictions and at all levels of government in the United States. If the behavior is threatening, the punishment is some form of loss of freedom through isolation. Schools suspend or expel students. Businesses fire employees. Cities, counties, and states put people in jail. The ultimate isolation is the death sentence.

Before I go on to talk about consequences, punishment, and jail, I'd like to clear up a point. Getting arrested is different from going to jail. Anyone can get arrested just by being in the wrong place at the wrong time. Innocent people are arrested every day. Being arrested only means you are suspected of committing a crime. Being arrested is frightening, embarrassing, and extremely inconvenient, to say the least, especially if you are detained and have to spend some time behind bars. But you don't go to jail, in the sense I am using the word, until you are tried, found guilty, and sentenced. When I talk about bringing teenagers back to the mainstream before they wind up dead or in jail, the jail I am talking about is the one you go to after you have been convicted and sentenced.

Which of the two types of consequences, direct or indirect, do you think would be most effective in getting teenagers to doubt their ability to continue surviving on the street? A lot of people would say indirect. They'd say, "If you want teenagers living on the street to start thinking that maybe they can't survive on the street, if you want them to really understand they're going to wind up dead or in jail, what better way than to put them in jail? That shows them they can't avoid going to jail. How are they going to tell you they won't wind up in jail when there they are sitting in jail? Right?" You'd think so, wouldn't you?

Unfortunately, it doesn't work that way. We put more people per capita in jail in the United States than any other industrialized nation in the world and we still have more crime than any other industrialized nation. In addition, most of the people we let out of jail wind up back there. So obviously, people in jail aren't learning that crime doesn't pay. If jails, sometimes called the universities of the street, teach them anything at all it's how to commit more crimes. If they come out of jail motivated to change their lives in any way, it's to be more careful and not get caught the next time.

Don't get me wrong here. I am not suggesting for a minute we don't need jails. They are an absolute necessity. If we can't convince the people living on the street to come back to the mainstream we need to lock them up so they can't continue to cause us harm. But remember our goal. It wasn't to punish teenagers for breaking the law and it wasn't to isolate them from the mainstream so they could no longer cause us harm, which are the two things jails do. Our goal was to bring them back to the mainstream before they wound up dead or in jail. If that is, in fact, our goal, then punishing them by putting them in jail is "killing the pig."

I must digress for a moment to explain this last phrase. When I was in my midteens, it was recommended to my family that I join something called the Farm Cadets. This was a New York State program that sent city kids to work on farms for the summer. So, in June of my fourteenth year, I found myself working on a dairy farm up near the Saint Lawrence Seaway, which was on the moon as far as I was concerned. Actually, the animals fascinated me and I was a tough kid and saw the hard work as a challenge.

One day we put up an electric fence to make a temporary pasture for the young cows, or heifers. We had Jersey cows that gave very rich milk and we sold some of that milk to the co-op and the rest of it to a local dairy. Another farmer, named Ben, who lived up the road, picked up the milk for the dairy every morning. The morning after we had put up the electric fence Ben came by and got to jawing with the farmer I worked for, whose name was Luther. Luther was a very good, kind, hardworking man in his sixties who always treated me with respect and for whom I worked very hard. Ben, on the other hand, was a few sandwiches short of a picnic.

Ben says, "I see you put up a 'lectric fence." "Yup. Thought I'd give it try," Luther replied. "I had me one a them onest," continued Ben. "I had me this pig would rut my yard up somethin' awful. So I put up one a them fences." (That's how they talked, honest.) "How'd it work," asked Luther. "Didn't," said Ben. "Pig knocked it down and went right on about his rutin'." "Oh," said Luther, somewhat concerned that we had wasted a day putting up our fence. Ben saw his concern and quickly added, "But I fixed it. Got rid a that damn box and plugged the whar right into the wall." "What happened?" asked Luther. "Well," said Ben with a big smile of satisfaction, "that ol' pig went up against the whar and it kilt the sum-a-bitch dead, right on the spot."

Now you have to understand I was a city kid and I didn't know much about farming. I had been standing there listening the whole time and the logic of Ben's solution escaped me. I did know what good manners were even though I didn't usually use them in the city, but this wasn't the city and I wasn't as sure of myself, so I said, "Excuse me, Ben. Why did you do that?" I glanced over at Luther to see if I was out of line and the expression on his face seemed to me to suggest he thought that was a pretty fair question, so I looked to Ben like I expected an answer. And he gave me one, one I've never forgotten. "Well," he said smugly, "I sure as hell taught that pig a lesson now din't I? He'll never rut my yard up again."

Poor Ben missed the point. Killing the pig didn't teach it to behave. It kept it from misbehaving. That's what jail does. That's not what we want to do. We want to teach teenagers to behave appropriately, not keep them from misbehaving. We don't want to "kill the pig."

So, if punishment, meaning loss of freedom by isolation from the mainstream, doesn't teach teenagers to behave appropriately, that leaves us with direct consequences. How does imposing the direct consequences of street behavior get us where we want to go?

Do you remember when I was describing what it was like to live in the street society and I said you can't care about anybody or anything but yourself because it makes you soft and being soft can get you killed? That's the chink in teenagers' armor. That's the way we get to them.

People on the street suppress their feelings of sympathy and compassion so they won't care about anything or anybody but themselves. These are the feelings that help shape a person's conscience. Another way of describing what they do is they push these feelings way down inside themselves and surround them with a hard shell so they no longer feel sympathy or compassion and no longer hear their conscience. That's where the street term "hard" comes from. When you say someone on the street is "hard," you're saying the shell they've built around their feelings and their conscience is impenetrable. Nothing can get through it. The "hardened criminal" is a criminal who feels nothing for others and cares about nothing but himself or herself.

It takes time to build up that shell, to make it really hard and impenetrable, and teenagers haven't had much time to do that. Most of them haven't been on the street for very long and none of them have been thinking for themselves for very long. Their minds are still fresh and young. They are still vulnerable and reachable. The shell they have started building around their feelings and their conscience is not that hard yet. As they get older that shell will get harder and they won't be as vulnerable or reachable anymore. That's why it is so important to get to them while they are still young. The older and harder they get, the more difficult it is to bring them back to the mainstream alive.

Here's how it works. Every time teenagers have to experience the direct consequences of their street behavior, every time they have to undo the harm they've done, they are connected to all the powerful feelings the harm they've caused has generated in others . . . feelings of loss, shame, embarrassment, frustration, anger, fear, pain, grief, etc. Making this connection is important because it exposes teenagers to these feelings and makes it obvious to them that they are responsible for these feelings because they caused them. Teenagers will try to reject these feelings and dismiss the notion that they are responsible for them because they know if they start to care they won't be able to do the kinds of things they have to do to survive on the street. But the feelings won't go away. They'll circle around in the teenagers' heads. And the notion that they are responsible for causing them will gnaw away at that shell. Each time they have to experience the direct consequences of their behavior, the feelings will grow stronger and the gnawing will increase in intensity. Eventually, because street teenagers aren't as "hard" as they'd like us to believe they are, it will all start to get to them. The feelings will start to get through the shell and the sense of being responsible for causing those feelings will turn into guilt and plague them. They'll start to care, and when that happens, they will begin to doubt their ability to continue surviving on the street. And the moment that happens, they will lose their nerve.

That moment is critical. If there is someone around they trust who can show them the way out, the way back to the mainstream, they might be willing to go. If there isn't someone they can trust around who is willing to help them, well, it isn't likely they will find their way back to the mainstream by themselves. They'll be trapped on the street and they'll be scared because they've lost their nerve and they'll start to get desperate. Desperation on the street is the fast lane that takes you straight to that dead end we keep talking about—death or jail.

If you start this process of imposing the direct consequences of street behavior, you have to make certain you are there when the teenagers in your life start to care, lose their nerve, and need your help. That can be difficult to do because there is no way to predict how long it will take for that to happen. It could be a week. It could be several years. You have to be prepared to stick it out.

Here's the best part. If you have been consistently and persistently imposing the direct consequences of street behavior and requiring the teenagers in your life to experience those consequences by making things right, fixing what they broke, replacing what they've taken, compensating people for the harm they've caused, and it has finally gotten through their shell; if they are starting to care, to lose their nerve, to look for a way to get off the street; and if they are willing to let you help them because they trust you . . . guess what? They are already halfway back to the mainstream. All that time they spent experiencing the direct consequences of their street behavior, having to undo the harm they have done, they didn't realize it, but they weren't just experiencing the direct consequences of their street behavior, they were practicing the skills they need to be successful in the mainstream. That's how you succeed in the mainstream. You succeed by doing the right thing, and that's exactly what they have been learning to do this whole time.

Now, here's the tricky part. In order for teenagers to undo the harm they've done, they have to do something positive—and remember, you can't make them do anything they don't want to do. So, this is how you work it. You offer them the opportunity to experience the direct consequences of their behavior as an alternative to having to experience the indirect consequences. In other words, you give them a chance to make things right instead of being punished. Naturally, you hope they choose to make things right because that is going to be more effective in terms of getting them back to the mainstream alive. But even if they don't, and you have to go ahead and impose punishment, you gain a couple of things that you wouldn't gain if you just imposed punishment straight out without offering the alternative.

First, you maintain your nonthreatening relationship. Even if you are the one who eventually suspends them from school or calls the police, they will know you tried to prevent that from happening. You offered them an alternative. You tried to help. You were not out to get them. You were not the enemy.

Second, punishment becomes less arbitrary and more like a direct consequence when they choose it and that brings them face to face with the notion of responsibility. They can't blame somebody else for punishing them when they brought the punishment on themselves by refusing the alternative. That makes them responsible for whatever suffering the punishment may cause them. That still doesn't accomplish as much as having to undo the harm they've done, but it's something and something is always better than nothing.

The bottom line here is teenagers must experience the consequences of their street behavior, one way or the other, by choosing to make things right or by choosing punishment. You don't control the former, but you do control the latter. So, there is no excuse for you letting the teenagers in your life get away with not experiencing the consequences of their street behavior. If you do let them get away with it, you are enabling them to continue surviving on the street and you will not get them back to the mainstream.

Let's look at an example and see how this all actually works.

Let's say you coach a high-school girls' basketball team. Your team is playing in a holiday invitational tournament.

During the tournament, someone sees one of your players stealing a warm-up suit from another team and reports it to the tournament officials who, in turn, confront you with the problem. The witness can't identify the person who took the warm-up suit because she only saw the person from the back, but she knows the thief was from your team because the thief was wearing one of your uniforms.

How would you handle something like that? Search all the girls' lockers and gym bags? Threaten to pull the team out of the tournament unless the guilty person steps forward? Tell the tournament officials you don't believe them and they can call the police if they want to? These are all possible reactions.

If you were trying to use the Streetwise Strategy, here's what you might do. We'll assume you already have a non-threatening relationship with the young ladies on your team. They know you're the coach and you're in charge, but they also know you care about them as people, not just about winning basketball games. So, you'd call a private team meeting off in a corner somewhere—no parents, boyfriends, etc. Just you and the members of the team. You'd describe the problem and explain how the incident embarrasses the school, the team, and you personally. You explain how it casts a shadow over the team's play. You also explain that if the uniform is not returned, the team could be suspended from the tournament. It will certainly jeopardize the school's chances of being invited back to the tournament in the future. You then tell the team members that you would like the young lady who took the warm-up suit to return it to you within the next half hour. You explain that if she does so she will not be kicked off the team. You go on to say this is a fairly serious problem, but it can be corrected and you want to do that before it becomes very serious and can't be corrected. You also say you will leave the van open in the parking lot. If the person who took the warm-up suit is not comfortable admitting to you she did it, you hope she would at least care enough about her teammates not to want to embarrass them or risk having them suspended from the tournament and would leave the warm-up suit in the van. Finally, you tell the young ladies if they know who took the warm-up suit, you would appreciate their trying to convince that person to do the right thing. Then you wait the half hour.

If you haven't gotten the warm-up suit back, or if you have but the person who took it left it in the van instead of coming to you, then you talk with each of the team members individually and ask them to tell you what they know and help you resolve the outstanding issues. If all the issues aren't resolved during the tournament, you start the process all over again when you get back to your own school.

What does this approach accomplish? First, it confirms your nonthreatening relationship. It is clear you are not out to get anyone. You are just trying to help solve a problem. Second, it is the only chance you have of getting the warm-up suit back and saving the team's, and the school's, reputation. It also positions you to use positive peer pressure to get the problem resolved. The members of the team who didn't take the warm-up suit will see that you gave the thief a face-saving way out. If they know what she's done, they will encourage her to do the right thing, or even insist on it. If she doesn't do the right thing, resulting in the team being suspended from the tournament or otherwise casting a shadow over the team's reputation, her teammates are not going to be very sympathetic toward her. At that point, they are much more likely to tell you what they know when you talk to them individually.

In a situation like this, if you use this approach and stay with it, the chances are you will get the warm-up suit back and find out who took it. You may not find out in thirty minutes, but you will later that day or after the tournament is over and you get back to your own school. There is no guarantee this will happen, but there is a very good chance it will. If you don't use this approach, it's pretty certain you won't get the warm-up suit back or find out who took it.

Now let's assume this works. The warm-up suit is returned by a girl named Sandy who admits she took it and says she is sorry. What do you do with her? How do you ensure she experiences the consequences of her behavior? Should she be kicked off the team? You promised not to do that if she returned the warm-up suit, and she did. You can't go back on your word. None of the young ladies on the team will ever trust you again. What if her friends returned the warm-up suit and told you Sandy took it? Now you wouldn't be breaking your word. Should you go ahead and kick her off the team? You could, but that's "killing the pig."

Kicking her off the team is justified, especially in the second instance where she didn't come forward and her teammates turned her in. It is a consequence of her stealing the warm-up suit. The problem with doing that is its punishment. It says to her, "You broke the law so we don't want you around anymore." It's the same as putting her in jail in the sense that it deprives her of the opportunity to participate as a member of the basketball team and it isolates her from her friends, the team, and all that goes with interscholastic athletics—prestige, a chance at a college scholarship, and the like. She suffers, of course. She definitely loses out, but she doesn't really have to face up to the real harm she has done, which was betray your trust and the trust of her teammates. The other problem with kicking her off the team is that doesn't give her a chance to undo what she did, to earn back your trust and the trust of her teammates. It pushes her further into the street instead of giving her a way back to the mainstream, and that, after all, is the goal here.

Another option would be to suspend her from the team for two weeks or a month. That's really no different from kicking her off the team. It's still punishment, just less severe. It still isolates her from the team and doesn't require her to undo what she did.

The course of action that is most consistent with the Streetwise Strategy is this: you tell her you will let her stay on the team, with certain conditions, provided she apologize publicly to her teammates and they agree to let her continue to be a part of the team. Sandy's teammates are likely to agree with this plan, especially if you explain the plan to them beforehand. Other conditions that Sandy will have to agree to are:

1. Come to practice every day and participate fully as a member of the team.
2. Come to all the games and suit up, but she won't be allowed to play in any of the games for a period of time. When her friends, who aren't on the team, see her suited up and sitting on the bench and want to know why, it will be up to her to decide what to tell them.
3. Show you and her teammates she cares enough about the team that you can trust she won't embarrass you by breaking the law again.

Until all three of the conditions are met, Sandy won't get to play in a game. If she doesn't work hard in practice because she knows she isn't going to get to play in the games, if she sits on the bench and sulks or criticizes her teammates because she thinks she can do better, if she doesn't show you and her teammates she can be trusted by being trustworthy, she won't get to play.

If she gets frustrated or angry along the way or begins to falter, you sit down and talk with her again. You put the whole situation back in perspective. You encourage her and support her and tell her you believe she can make it back and that you want her to make it back. You take it one day at a time, and when she makes it back and the team says they feel comfortable letting her play again, you all celebrate Sandy's making it back and the incident is over, never to be brought up again. If she is unwilling to accept this alternative or doesn't keep up her part of the bargain, then she is kicked off the team. Sandy gets to make the decision. She can make things right or she can accept the punishment. One way or the other, she has to experience the consequences of her behavior.

Keep in mind that sometimes the harm teenagers cause when they break the law is to themselves. That doesn't change anything. They still have to experience the consequences of their behavior if you want to get them back to the mainstream. They should be offered the opportunity to make things right, and if they refuse to do so, then they should have to endure the punishment.

Here's an example.

You first found out your son was involved with drugs when he was fifteen years old. He was riding in a car with some older boys. The police stopped the car and found marijuana in it and took all the boys down to the police station. The police couldn't prove the drugs belonged to your son or that he had used them, so they had to let him go. He was arrested again a year later at the mall. This time he had marijuana in his possession and was sentenced to probation on the condition he get counseling.

He went for counseling, but it didn't do much good. He became very moody and lost interest in most things, including school. Finally, a month into his senior year, he quit school. He was seventeen years old. You were very upset about that, but he told you he had gotten a good job in an auto body shop. He went to work every day and brought some money home at the end of the week, so you thought it was okay. What you didn't know was that his job was to steal cars for the body shop, called a chop shop, which took them apart and sold the parts. You also didn't know he developed a methamphetamine (crank) habit. The money he brought home was only a little of what he made. He was spending most of the money he made on his drugs. Two months ago, shortly after he turned nineteen, he was arrested a third time, this time for possession of methamphetamines. You were relieved when the judge gave him probation with the stipulation that he get treatment. Since he'd been on probation once before, you were sure they were going to throw the book at him. But the police didn't know he was stealing cars, and the judge didn't know he was hurting other people. The judge saw your son's drug problem as an illness that caused him to break the law. The judge believed your son and the mainstream would be better served if he went to a local residential drug treatment center instead of to jail. The judge made it very clear, however, that if your son didn't complete treatment, he would go to jail for at least two years. You didn't want to see him go to jail and you prayed the treatment program would get him straightened out.

Your son has been at the treatment center almost thirty days. Today, a counselor from the center called to tell you your son hasn't been cooperative. He has denied having a problem the whole time he's been there, and this afternoon he walked off the center. The counselor expected your son to come to see you and asked that you bring him back to the center if he showed up at your door. She went on to say that if he didn't come back, she'd have to notify the court and it would, in all probability, revoke his probation.

It's now about eight o'clock. It is a very cold February night and, sure enough, your son comes knocking at your door. If you want to impose the consequences of his behavior, the conversation might go like this.

SON: Hi.

YOU: Hi. I was expecting you. Your counselor at the treatment center called and said you'd walked out. She thought you might come here. Why did you leave there?

SON: That place is not for me. It's for drug addicts and people with serious problems. I'm not a drug addict. They told me I didn't need that kind of program.

YOU: That's interesting, because that's not what your counselor told me when she called here.

SON (*annoyed and embarrassed that you'd caught him in an outright lie*): What did they you tell you?

YOU (*calm but firm*): They said you needed to go back, that you needed help.

SON: Oh, I can explain that. (*Then noticing he is still standing on the doorstep*) Aren't you going to let me in?

YOU: No, I'm afraid not. I'd be happy to drive you back to the treatment center because I believe they can help you, but I'm not letting you back into the house until you get this drug thing straightened out.

SON (*Going into his "getting over" act—Scene 1, The Sympathy Game*): You don't understand what it's like there. They lock you in your room, they don't let you do anything, the food is horrible, and this one guy gets his jollies by punching on you every chance he gets. I can't go back there.

YOU: I don't really believe that, but even if it were true, you're old enough to make your own decisions and old enough to accept responsibility for those decisions. You chose to use drugs, now you have to live with the consequences. The judge said if you don't complete the program at the treatment center he is going to lock you up. I'm sure that would be a lot worse than the treatment center.

SON (*Scene 2, The Guilt Trip*): That's not fair. This is all your fault. If you'd had a little more time for me none of this would have ever happened. But, no, you were always too busy with your damned job and showing off to your friends. You never had time for me. I wouldn't be in this mess if it wasn't for you. You owe me.

YOU: I know I've made some mistakes and I'm sorry about that. I really would do things differently if I had it to do over again. But I don't and I'm not the one who was using drugs. You did that to yourself.

SON (*Scene 3, The Big Threat*): I hate you. If you don't let me in, you'll never see me again. I swear, you'll never see me again.

YOU: I'd be very sad if I never saw you again and I hope that doesn't happen, but I'm not letting you in. It's because I do want to see you again that I'm doing this. You need to go back to the treatment center.

SON (*Scene 4, The Desperate Plea*): Please, I'm begging you. Let me stay here, just for tonight. I'm tired and I'm freezing and I can't even think straight. I have nowhere else to go. It's twenty

degrees out here. If you don't let me in I'll freeze
to death.

YOU: You do have somewhere else to go. Two places
really. You can go back to the treatment center or
you can go to jail. You don't have to freeze to
death. Wait here. I'll get my coat and the cars keys
and I'll drive you back to the treatment center. We
can talk some more in the car.

At this point, you close the door and get your coat and
keys. Will your son still be there when you open the door
again? There is no way to know. If he is, it's a good sign.
It means he is starting to doubt his ability to survive on
the street, he is starting to lose his nerve, and that's the
first step back to the mainstream. If he isn't there, then he
must still think he can find a way to survive.

I know it would be very, very hard to come back to
the door with your coat on and your keys in your hand
and see your son running off down the block. You'll want
to call after him, or get in the car and go after him. You'll
want to bring him back to the house and feed him and let
him get a good night's sleep. You'll hope that the next
morning you can talk some sense into him. You won't. All
you will do is confirm what he already believes, which is
that he can continue to use drugs and avoid the consequences. You will enable him to continue surviving on the
street and, by doing so, greatly diminish his chances of getting off the street. You must let him go. You must tell
yourself that you have done the best thing you could do
by offering him an alternative, a way back to the mainstream. You didn't tell him you didn't want to see him
again until he was off drugs. You offered to help. You
offered to take him back to the treatment center. If he
chooses not to accept your help, not to make things right,

then he will either freeze to death or go to jail. It is the only hope you have of bringing him back to the mainstream alive.

Let's look at a few more examples to help you get the hang of offering teenagers the opportunity to experience the direct consequences of their street behavior as an alternative to being punished.

You run the recreation program at a boarding school, a Job Corps center, or a similar residential facility where students live and attend classes on campus. Mario has been coming in almost every night for about six months to lift weights. He is a big, strong, very likeable seventeen-year-old. The other young men who use the weight room look up to him. This past week another young man started coming around to use the weights. His name is Arthur. He's a tall, skinny fifteen-year-old with a big mouth. He doesn't know what he's doing and has been getting in everyone's way and on everyone's nerves. Arthur comes to you and tells you the guys in the weight room have been threatening him all week, especially Mario, and today Mario pushed him against the wall and tried to choke him. Arthur says he wants to lift weights, but he's afraid to go back into the weight room because of Mario.

You tell Arthur you'll look into the situation and, in the meantime, he's to stay away from the weight room. Then you call Mario into your office and ask him to tell you his side of the story. Mario explains Arthur doesn't know what he's doing. He has dropped weights several times and almost hurt some people. When someone tries to explain the weight room rules or tell him how to lift correctly, he has a smart answer for them. Mario admits to threatening Arthur but insists he didn't hurt him.

Here's how you might respond to this situation using the Streetwise Strategy. First, you explain to Mario that

Arthur's big mouth is just his way of covering up his fear. He knows he doesn't know what he's doing and he's afraid of looking stupid, so he talks like he's a "big man" who knows "what's up" in the hope that no one will notice he's afraid. Then you remind Mario that he didn't know what he was doing and had a bit of chip on his shoulder himself when he first started lifting weights, but someone was willing to look past his attitude and take the time to show him what to do. Finally, you explain that Mario should have come to you and told you about the problems everyone was having with Arthur instead of taking matters into his own hands. His actions were unacceptable and he will now have to "live with the consequences."

You might present what you have in mind to Mario this way:

"I've talked to Arthur and I believe he really wants to learn to lift weights, but now he is not only afraid of looking stupid, he's afraid of getting hurt because of what you did to him. In order to undo what you've done, I want you to be Arthur's big brother. I want you to look after him and make sure no one messes with him. And I want you to show him how to lift. I'm going to hold you responsible for Arthur. If anything happens to him, you could lose your privileges to use the weight room."

Mario will most certainly object, "That's not fair."

"I think it is," you reply. "If you'd come to me instead of pushing Arthur around, he wouldn't be afraid to go back into the weight room and he wouldn't need someone to look out for him."

Mario will probably think about what you just said for a moment and then ask, "But what am I supposed to do when he opens his big mouth? I can't deal with that."

"Sure you can," you reply. "Take him aside, privately, and just call him on it. Tell him you know he talks big to cover up being afraid and he doesn't have to because it's okay to be afraid. Tell him how you felt when you first started lifting. If he keeps talking trash tell him, 'Hey, do you want to learn to lift, or not? I'm willing to show you and I'm the best there is around here, but you've got to keep your big mouth shut.' It may take a little while but I'm sure he'll come around. You're a natural leader, Mario, and I'm sure if you give Arthur a chance, he'll follow your lead."

If Mario agrees, and he will because he doesn't want to be banned from the weight room, then you bring Arthur and Mario together and explain to Arthur that Mario will look after him but he has to do as Mario says. Want to bet Mario and Arthur become the best of friends in a matter of weeks?

Here's another example.

Your fourteen-year-old daughter spent Saturday night at a pajama party with some girlfriends. Sunday morning the mother of the girl who held the party calls you to tell you she caught the girls smoking marijuana the previous night. She explains she didn't actually see them smoking, but she smelled it and found what was left of a "joint" in the ashtray. You wait for your daughter and when she arrives home you have a talk. Your daughter immediately breaks into tears. "I'm sorry, Mama. I didn't know there would be drugs at the party. I didn't smoke any. Honest. It was this one girl I didn't even know who brought it."

This is a little tricky. If you call your daughter a liar and she isn't lying, you undermine your nonthreatening relationship with her and teach her it doesn't pay to tell the truth because you won't believe her anyway. If she is lying and you don't do anything, then she gets away with smoking marijuana and lying.

Here's one way to handle this kind of situation. First of all, you explain that even if she didn't smoke any of the marijuana herself, she has some responsibility for what happened. She could have told her friend's mother what was going on or called and told you. As a result of her not doing that, you can no longer completely trust her or her friends. Since you can no longer trust her or her friends, she will only be allowed to socialize with those same girls at your house when you are at home so you can keep an eye on them. The alternative is she won't be allowed to socialize with them at all. This won't guarantee that your daughter won't smoke marijuana with her friends after school, but it does require her to experience the direct consequences of being at that particular party and not doing anything to stop what was happening, and that consequence is the loss of your trust.

I said earlier, when I was talking about prevention, it is fair to assume a teenager who is breaking rules is capable of breaking the law. The same can be said for imposing the consequences of inappropriate behavior. You don't have to wait until teenagers are breaking the law to impose the consequences of their behavior. There are consequences for breaking rules, too. Although the direct and indirect consequences for breaking rules are generally not as severe as those associated with breaking the law, you can still impose them. The punishment imposed for breaking rules can be very unpleasant and teenagers may well prefer to have the opportunity to make things right rather than be punished.

By imposing the direct consequences of all inappropriate behavior you keep teenagers in touch with their feelings. That makes it harder for them to bury those feelings and build a shell around them. It also helps them understand that they are responsible for their own actions. In fact, always imposing the consequences of inappropriate behavior can actually help prevent many teenagers from ever going to the street. Not doing so, or doing so only some of the time, actually encourages and maintains inappropriate behavior. It says to teenagers that the behavior is okay, or that it is okay some of the time.

Here's another example. This one involves confronting the consequences of breaking a rule.

You are the assistant principal at a middle school. Four students get into a food fight in the cafeteria during lunch and make a mess of the place. By the time they get to your office and you sort out what happened, it's too late to have them clean up the mess they made, which is the most obvious direct consequence of their behavior, because the cafeteria staff already did that. However, the cafeteria workers aren't the only people who were affected by the food fight. All the other students in the cafeteria at the time, especially those that got food all over them, had their lunch ruined by the commotion. So, why not have the culprits pay their classmates' back for the lunch they ruined by requiring them to make their classmate's lunch extra special for the next week by bussing tables and taking everyone's tray back to the dirty tray window? A public apology might be in order, as well. The alternative, of course, is detention or a parent conference.

Do you see how this works? Every time teenagers exhibit inappropriate behavior, whether it's breaking the rules or breaking the law, you need to find a way to give them the opportunity to experience the direct consequences of their behavior, to make things right. If they choose not to take advantage of that opportunity, then you have to make sure that the appropriate punishment is imposed. You will be tempted to go straight to the punishment or to do nothing at all. You need to resist those temptations. People who don't understand what you are doing may criticize you. Some will say you are being too soft and others will say you are being to hard. Thank them for their concern, but don't be swayed by their opinions. Imposing the consequences of inappropriate behavior is the right thing to do. It is what works.

There is one more benefit of imposing the consequences of all inappropriate behavior in the manner I have described. While teenagers are learning that they can't avoid the consequences of their behavior, they are also learning that they can change those consequences by changing their behavior. It can happen suddenly or over a period of time, but eventually teenagers begin to understand that if they do things right in the first place, then they won't have to make them right in the second place, and therein lies the beginning of wisdom. It is also the jumping-off point for redirecting a teenagers talents and abilities, which is the next step in the Streetwise Strategy.

Redirecting Talents and Abilities

We are each born with unique talents and abilities. If we live in the mainstream, we use these talents and abilities to develop the skills we need to succeed. If we live on the street, we use them to develop the skills we need to survive. The talents and abilities are the same; it is how they are used that is different. In the mainstream, the skills are used within the law. On the street, the skills are used without regard for the law. Not all of the skills developed to survive on the street are directly transferable to the mainstream, but many of them are. It is important to understand this point because the final step in bringing teenagers back to the mainstream alive involves helping them identify the talents and abilities they have been using to survive on the street and showing them how to use those same talents and abilities to be successful in the mainstream. It also involves giving them credit for the skills they have developed on the street when those skills are transferable to the mainstream.

While I have called this the final step, you can actually take this step anytime. The moment you recognize that the teenagers you live or work with are on the street, you can look for the talents and abilities they are using to "get over" and show them how they could use those same talents and abilities to "make it" in the mainstream. It can never hurt to try. However, redirecting talents and abilities will be most effective when teenagers have started to care, have lost their nerve, and are looking for a way off the street.

Redirection is a very exciting and rewarding process. There is much satisfaction in seeing a teenager make the connection and then make the adjustment. In order to do this, you first have to rid yourself of the preconception that street behavior is so repulsive that nothing about it can be worthwhile or worth salvaging. You have to be able to see past the unlawful acts to recognize and appreciate the talents and abilities it takes to commit those acts. It is very upsetting to have someone pick your wallet out of your purse without your noticing, but think how nimble that person's fingers must be in order to do that. Wouldn't someone with such nimble fingers make an excellent jeweler or electronic assembler?

You also have to look at the skills teenagers have developed on the street and, where those skills are transferable to the mainstream, you have to make every effort to give them credit for having developed those skills when they get to the mainstream.

For example, a teenager with leadership ability, who has developed leadership skills and has become a leader on the street, should be offered the opportunity to be a leader in the mainstream. You can't say to a gang leader, "Come to the mainstream and prove yourself. With your leadership abilities and skills, I am sure you will become a leader there as well." Wait a minute. She (it could also be a he, but let's assume this particular gang leader is a she) is already a leader. What do you mean by "become a leader?" Does that mean she won't be a leader when she gets to the mainstream? If she is not a leader, the only thing left to be is a follower. Why would she want to give up being a leader to become a follower? And what exactly is it you want her to prove? Her leadership ability? She's already done that. Leading on the street is the same as leading in the mainstream. The only difference is the law—remember? So what does she have to prove, her trustworthiness? She can do that just as easily from a position of leadership as she can as a follower. If she gets credit in the mainstream for the leadership skills she has developed on the street, the transition from street to mainstream will be a lateral move, and a lateral move is easier to make. If she has to go backward before she can go forward, she is less likely to want to make the move and less likely to be successful in the mainstream if she does make it.

Here's another example.

You are dealing with a young man who steals cars. He has used his mechanical talents and abilities to develop some very sophisticated automotive skills and, consequently, is very good at what he does. In fact, he has worked his way up to stealing luxury cars for sale on the black market overseas. He found out recently that a classic Mercedes he stole belonged to an old lady whose husband had left it to her when he died. It turns out that the car was really all she had. She couldn't afford to insure it and she never drove it. She was holding on to it as an investment, hoping that it would continue appreciating in value so that, if she got sick or could no longer take care of herself, she could sell it to help pay her medical expenses.

The young man found all this out from a girl he was dating. She didn't know he was a car thief and she was telling him this story about an old lady that had been her grandmother's best friend and about how devastated and frightened the old lady was now that her car had been stolen because she didn't have any family to help her. He casually asked where the old lady lived and realized that it was he who had stolen her car. The story really bothered the young man. He had always felt he wasn't really hurting anyone because he was stealing from the rich and they could afford to buy new cars. It was too late to return the car to its owner. It had already been sold, but the young man felt badly for the old lady. As it dawned on him that his unlawful behavior was actually hurting other people, as he started feeling for other people and caring what happened to them, he started to lose his nerve. Now he is looking for a way off the street and he comes to you for advice because he trusts you. You could be a relative, a former teacher, a minister—just about anybody he trusts. He tells you the whole story and asks you to help him get a legitimate job so he won't have to steal anymore to meet his needs.

You could say, "Well, you obviously have mechanical abilities and have developed some good automotive skills. I have a friend who owns a garage. You could probably get a job there. You'd have to start out pumping gas and changing tires, but I'm sure you could work your way up quickly." Wrong! This young man already knows how to bypass fancy alarm systems on the most expensive cars. How long do you think it would take him to learn how to install them? And wouldn't it be of value to a company that installs car alarms to have someone working for them who knows how to bypass them? He might even be able to show them ways to make their alarms more tamper proof. Helping this young man get a job where he could learn to install car alarms would be giving him credit in the mainstream for the skills he developed on the street. It would be a lateral move. Pumping gas and changing flat tires would be going backward before he could go forward.

I have intentionally chosen these two examples because I know they raise some serious concerns. I know someone is going to say, "Now wait a minute. Are you telling us we should give criminals positions of responsibility in the mainstream? These people can't be trusted. What's to keep a gang leader who becomes a student leader in high school from using her authority to sell drugs to the other high school students? What's to keep a car thief who is installing car alarms from rigging them so it is easier for him to steal the cars after they've left the shop? I'm sorry. This is going too far."

If this is what you are saying or thinking, it is quite understandable. These are legitimate concerns and they need to be addressed. What exactly is it that you don't trust about the gang leader and the car thief? Do you not trust their skills? Do you believe the gang leader can't lead and won't be able to get others to follow? Do you believe the car thief doesn't know anything about car alarms and won't be able to make them work when he installs them in your car? Probably not. My guess is you are not questioning their skills. What you don't trust is their ability to apply those skills within the limits set by the mainstream's laws. I wouldn't either. That's right, I said I wouldn't trust their ability to apply their skills within the limits set by the mainstream's laws. Therefore, what I would do is set up some tight controls that would allow me to monitor how they applied their skills in the mainstream. What I wouldn't do is deprive them of the opportunity to use their skills in the mainstream.

Do you see the difference? If the former gang leader became a student leader in your school, you'd have to watch what she did much more closely than you would have to watch someone else who came from the main-stream. If the former car thief were installing car alarms in your shop, you'd have to check his work more closely and more frequently than you would have to check the work of someone who came from the mainstream. But you shouldn't require the gang leader or the car thief to abandon their skills in order to earn your trust, not if you really want them to come back to the mainstream.

This brings up another concern. Someone else is bound to say, "Wait a minute. These people screwed up. They broke the law. What's wrong with making them start over again from square one? There are lots of kids who never broke the law. They have to start out pumping gas. Why should criminals get a break?" This is also a legiti-mate concern. I'm not suggesting our gang leader and car thief be given the opportunities I've described in the two examples because they were criminals. I am suggesting they have earned these opportunities because they have developed the necessary skills. If a mainstream teenager had the leadership skills of our hypothetical gang leader, she'd be a student leader. If a mainstream teenager knew as much about car alarms as our hypothetical car thief, he wouldn't be pumping gas, either. He'd be installing car alarms. You simply cannot deny teenagers the opportunity to use the skills they have developed by applying their tal-ents and abilities on the street, while at the same time expect them to succeed in the mainstream.

There is one more concern raised by these examples. Who is to say that the car thief wouldn't be good at something else totally unrelated to cars? Isn't it possible the car thief would be good at lots of other things not related to cars? Of course it is. However, in this particular example, the young man has mechanical talents and abilities he has already used to develop automotive skills. Why waste those skills? Why require that the young man develop another set of skills before he can begin to experience success in the mainstream? The quicker he can experience success in the mainstream, the quicker he finds he can meet his needs in the mainstream, the more likely he is to stay in the mainstream.

There is something else you need to know about street behavior that can help you redirect teenagers' talents and abilities so that they can succeed in the mainstream. As teenagers go through the process of differentiation, as they begin to develop a sense of themselves and minds of their own, they begin to recognize what they can do. That is to say, they begin to recognize their talents and abilities and they develop interests and skills based on those talents and abilities. Unfortunately, they aren't always allowed to pursue those interests or develop those skills in the mainstream. The mainstream has a tendency to lay its own trip on teenagers. Parents, relatives, teachers, guidance counselors, community leaders, and the media all seem to have expectations for the next generation. It has to do with all of us wanting our children to have better lives than we've had. So we encourage them, push them, manipulate them, and direct them to do the things that worked for us or the things we wish we had done. We do it out of love, but what we often fail to recognize is that what we want for our children, what the mainstream wants for its next generation, may not be what they want for themselves. As a result, mainstream teenagers often do not develop interests and skills based on their own inherent talents and abilities. They develop the interests and skills the mainstream says they should develop whether they have an aptitude for them or not, or they develop none at all.

Here is a classic example.

There was a young man who loved science. From his very first days in elementary school he was fascinated by everything that had to do with science. He read about science. He watched science shows on television. He even built his own weather station out of rubber balls and old bottles he found around the house. He made daily forecasts that were as accurate as the forecasts being made by the meteorologists on the local radio and television stations. But he wasn't very good at arithmetic. So, when he got to high school, his guidance counselor told him he wouldn't be allowed to take any science classes because, since he wasn't good at arithmetic, he couldn't, in the counselors' considered opinion, possibly succeed in science and the school didn't want to "set him up for failure." Unable to pursue his interests, the young man went through high school majoring in surfing and drugs. He barely graduated and went to work in the kitchen of a local hospital delivering trays to patients' rooms.

Fortunately, this story has a happy ending, although many similar stories don't. This young man's family encouraged him to take some classes at the local community college. He signed up for a statistics course because he thought it sounded interesting. He got an A in it. His professor felt he demonstrated the ability to develop higher math skills and urged him to take a calculus course. He got an A in that course, too. From there he went on to a four-year college where he earned a bachelor's degree in nuclear physics. He was awarded a full scholarship to the University of California at Berkeley, where he earned a master's degree in mechanical engineering. He now directs software development for a company that produces quality control equipment used in the manufacture of computer chips. He has a pilot's license, owns two airplanes (which he helps maintain himself), owns a yacht, owns some real estate, and is constantly approached by companies who want him to work for them. Boy, isn't he lucky his high-school guidance counselor didn't want to "set him up for failure"?

The street is very different from the mainstream in this respect. There is nobody to tell you what you should learn or what you should be able to do. There is no pressure to live up to anyone else's expectations. Teenagers are not only free to, they are forced to, use their unique talents and abilities to develop the skills they need to survive. There is no room for failure on the streets. There is no one to cover for you or make excuses for you. If you want to survive, you have to do what you are good at doing. You have to use your inherent talents and abilities. What this all means is that, while teenagers in the mainstream may or may not be using their unique talents and abilities to develop the skills they need to be successful in the mainstream, teenagers on the street are using their unique talents and abilities to develop the skills they need to survive.

It is not coincidence or chance that teenagers on the street do different things to get what they need and want. Teenagers do what they know they can do to "get over." They use their talents and abilities to develop specific skills they feel confident they can use to survive. You'll never see a fat purse-snatcher. Fat people can't run fast enough to snatch purses. They'll get caught. For similar reasons you won't see skinny, baby-faced bullies, ugly high-priced call girls, clumsy shoplifters, illiterate computer hackers, or con artists who don't have the gift of gab. You won't see them because they won't survive. They'll be dead or in jail.

Getting back to our gang leader, our car thief, and others like them, if they are surviving, you can be reasonably certain they are using their unique talents and abilities to do what they do best. And it is those unique talents and abilities, together with any transferable skills they have developed, which should be redirected to the mainstream.

It would take a very long time to list all the things teenagers do to survive, examine the talents and abilities required for each action, consider the skills they lead to, and then describe all the ways those talents, abilities, and skills could be redirected to the mainstream. Even then I'm sure I'd miss something. So I'm not even going to try. What I am going to do, however, is tie some of this information together to give you a sense of what you might look for in helping redirect the teenagers in your life from the street to the mainstream.

First let me say that teenage murderers, rapists, armed robbers, and kidnappers belong in jail. There is no place for them in the mainstream. A pyromaniac needs psychiatric care, but teenage arsonists who go out of their way to avoid hurting people and just seem to like to play with fire might find successful mainstream careers in pyrotechnics or fire fighting.

Muggers and enforcers on the street do well in contact sports like football and boxing, make good soldiers, can be very effective police officers or security guards, and can be successful doing some of the more physical and dangerous jobs that need to be done, like being a stevedore, a miner, or a lumberjack. Why? Because you have to be physically and mentally tough and unafraid of physical danger to survive as a mugger or enforcer on the street. And you need those same talents and abilities to be successful at these kinds of mainstream jobs.

Pimps are real interesting people. They get everyone else to take the risks and they make most of the money. Isn't that what the most successful real estate developers or investment brokers do?

Drug dealers are businessmen. They understand supply and demand, inventory control, marketing, accounting, and know how to leverage an investment and increase market share. A good drug dealer could run any kind of mainstream business.

Loan sharks are money managers operating without regard for the law. In the mainstream they'd do well in all aspects of banking, in securities and commodities trading, in economics, in finance, in fact, in anything that has to do with manipulating money, and a lot of what goes on in the mainstream has to do with manipulating money.

Sometimes people get offended when I start making these connections and I don't mean to offend anyone. Please understand I am not implying that real estate developers are pimps or that any of the other professions I've mentioned are less than honorable. I'm just pointing out that the talents and abilities real estate developers need to be successful in the mainstream are the same as the talents and abilities pimps need to survive on the street. There is no value judgment being made or suggested about real estate developers or any other profession. Nor am I trying to glorify street behavior. People's talents and abilities are what they have to work with to make a life for themselves. They are inherently neither good nor bad. It is how they are used that matters. Remember, you have to look past the criminal behavior, much of which may be reprehensible, to see the talents and abilities that can be redirected to the mainstream. That can be very hard to do sometimes, but you have to do it if you want to bring teenagers back to the mainstream alive.

Think for a moment about the cat burglar climbing up to a second-story window, slipping inside your house while you are asleep and stealing your wallet and watch from your night table without waking you up. It's a real scary thought, I know. But don't you think somebody with that kind of physical ability and nerve would make a great iron-worker or steeplejack building skyscrapers and bridges?

How about prostitution? It would be devastating to find out your daughter had become a prostitute and extremely difficult to look past the behavior to find the talents and abilities that could be redirected to the main-stream. Do you know what the difference is between a cheap whore and a high-class hooker? The cheap whore is not surviving. She is being used, hurt, and locked up with little or nothing to show for her troubles. She has very little worth taking to the mainstream, except perhaps her resilience. She's going to need a lot of tender loving care to rebuild her self-esteem before she can expect to be successful in the mainstream. The high-class hooker, on the other hand, is a prostitute who is surviving. She is making money and not getting hurt or going to jail. While she does sell her sexual favors, she does so on her terms. She is using her sexuality to get other people to do what she wants them to do. That's a talent and there is a place for it in the mainstream. Entertainers and models need it and use it. Sexuality is a big part of charm and charm is an asset to most jobs that require you to work with and influence other people, especially people of the opposite sex. If you see the talent and ability in teenagers for using their sexuality to get others to do what they want, those talents and abilities are worth redirecting.

Con artists and other types of hustlers have all kinds of talents and abilities that can be redirected to help them suc-ceed in the mainstream. They are resourceful, imaginative, articulate, and persuasive. They think quickly, improvise well, and are very sensitive to other people's needs (which they exploit, but that can be redirected). A good con artist or street hustler is almost guaranteed success if his or her talents and abilities can be redirected to mainstream careers in counseling, sales, public relations, or politics.

We've already talked about the car thief's mechanical abilities and how he has used them to develop automotive skills that are marketable in the mainstream. There are many other high tech skills that teenagers develop on the street and can be redirected to the mainstream. The computer hacker definitely has a career as a software developer or local area computer network (LAN) manager. A burglar who can circumvent a complicated security system would do well in electronics. And anyone who can pick locks is already a locksmith.

In the last chapter, I talked about "beating the rap" and explained how that was part of "getting over," or surviving on the street. Some people, regardless of which laws they break, get caught but don't do much jail time. They are arrested often but rarely get convicted. There are some talents and abilities involved in being able to do this; it isn't just luck. They figure out how the criminal justice system works and use their knowledge of the system to protect themselves from it. You guessed it—they'd make great lawyers.

Finally, there is the ability to think and function under pressure. Placing your freedom at risk or your life on the line is about as much pressure as anyone could ever have to face. Teenagers who have survived on the street, for even a short time, have learned how to handle that kind of pressure. The ability to think and function under pressure will be an asset in the mainstream no matter what a teenager chooses to do for a living.

As I said earlier, this list is not exhaustive. It is just meant to get you started looking for connections. You will have to identify the specific talents and abilities the teenagers in your life are using to survive on the street and determine for yourself, based on your own knowledge and experience, how they might be redirected so the teenagers can be successful in the mainstream. You will have to look closely at the skills teenagers have developed using their talents and abilities on the street and determine for yourself if and how they might be able to get credit for those skills in the mainstream. And you are going to have to sell the concept of redirection to teenagers so you have to understand it, be able to explain it, and believe in it.

Once you've identified the talents and abilities the teenagers you live with or work with are using to survive on the street and you've figured out how to redirect those talents and abilities to the mainstream, what exactly do you do?

First you tell them, then you show them, then you let them try it for themselves. Here is an example.

Let's assume your high-school age daughter has been working for a fast food chain after school and has been using the money she has been making to buy extra clothes. You start to notice some of the clothes she has been buying are fairly expensive. When you ask her about them, she tells you she's a good shopper and got them on sale. You are not satisfied with that explanation and one day, while she's out, you decide to snoop around her room. You are shocked to find a lot of expensive clothes in her closet. To make matters worse, you find a bag full of beautiful and very expensive clothes from an exclusive shop with the tags still on them and they are not even your daughter's size.

You confront your daughter when she comes home. You tell her you think the clothes in the bag are stolen. She denies it and says they belong to a friend. You suggest she return the clothes to the store, to make things right. She tells you you're crazy. You explain to her it is up to her to decide whether or not she wants to take the clothes back, but if she doesn't you will. "You can't do that," she says. "They belong to my friend." "Fine," you reply. "Have your friend come and pick them up. I'll hold them for her." "What if she decides she doesn't want them?" your daughter asks. "Then I'll return them to the store," you say calmly. There is a pause in the conversation as your daughter, realizing her bluff as been called, decides what to try next. "Okay," she says, "What if I did steal them? You mean you'd really turn me into the police?" "No," you say. "It's not my place to do that. The clothes don't belong to me. It's up to the store to decide whether they want to call the police or not."

You confiscate the items and give your daughter a couple of days to decide what she wants to do. She's angry with you at first. Then she comes to you and admits she stole the items and apologizes. "If you let me keep them, I'll never steal again. I promise," she pleads. "I'm sorry," you say. "You chose to take what didn't belong to you. Now you have to accept the consequences. You take them back or I do." This conversation is followed by a scene in which your daughter says she hates you and is leaving home. She does, in fact, pack a small bag and leave the house, but you find out that she's staying with a friend.

You return the clothes to the store and explain the situation to the security manager. He calls the police and they come to talk to you. They believe your daughter may be part of an exclusive shoplifting ring that has been stealing lots of expensive women's clothing from all of the better stores in town. The stolen clothes are then resold to other unsuspecting stores or individuals. The ring leaders are very clever and the young girls they recruit to steal the merchandise are so good and well trained that they haven't been able to catch any of the girls involved or identify the ring leaders. Your daughter could be the break they have been waiting for and they are willing to make a deal with your daughter if she'll cooperate with them and tell them what she knows about the operation.

You get in touch with your daughter and explain the situation. She's furious with you and refuses to talk to the police, so you tell the police where she is and have her arrested. You then get a lawyer to represent her and the lawyer gets her out on bail. The next several months are pure hell. The district attorney is threatening to throw the book at your daughter because she won't cooperate with the police. Her lawyer tells her she could be looking at serious jail time and recommends she tell the police what they want to know. She's almost ready to give in and then one of her friends, who was also part of the shoplifting ring, gives her a message from the ringleaders. "If you give them up, they say they'll hurt you bad."

Your daughter starts to get really scared. She's beginning to realize this isn't a game and she doesn't have what it takes to survive. She finally breaks down and tells the police all she knows, which is a lot. They move quickly and arrest a number of her fellow shoplifters. The ringleaders move their operation to another town and your daughter is put on probation. Now is the time to redirect her talents and abilities.

You begin by telling her the police told you she was a very good shoplifter and ask her to tell you how she stole the clothes and what made her so good at it. Now that you know she is no longer shoplifting, you should find her stories fascinating and encourage her to tell you all the "gory" details, just as if she were telling you about a party she went to. You'll probably learn that one thing that made her a good shoplifter was that she had very quick, sure hands. If she didn't, she would have dropped things or not have hidden them completely and gotten caught. And she had an excellent sense of fashion, which is how she knew what to take. Since she was working for a ring that resold the clothes she stole, she had to know what people would want to buy. Now that you know what you have to work with, you are ready to start redirecting.

First you tell her.

In this case, your daughter's actual shoplifting skills are not directly transferable to the mainstream. But her talents and abilities are, so you start by acknowledging those talents and abilities. You tell your daughter how valuable they are in the mainstream and you describe several ways in which they could be applied. I can see her doing well in fashion design or as a dressmaker or seamstress. I can even see a connection to cosmetology. It isn't clothes, but it is fashion and her quick, sure hands would be a real asset. Her hands wouldn't help her as a buyer or fashion coordinator for the retail industry, but her fashion sense would. You might be able to think of other connections.

Let's say, for the purpose of this example, she shows some interest in cosmetology by asking several questions about it, such as, "Why do you think I'd be a good hairstylist? Don't you have to go to school for that? How much money do hairstylists make?" That's your cue to move to the next step.

Then you show her.

You call a couple of the fanciest hair salons in town, explain that your daughter is interested in a career in cosmetology, and ask if you could bring her by to observe the very best in action. One, if not all, of the places you call is bound to say yes to that pitch. They'll not only show her around, I'm sure they will be happy to answer any questions she has.

If she is still showing some interest after the visit to the fancy hair salon, you take her to visit a cosmetology school, buy her some magazines on hairstyling, take some books out on the subject from the library and take her to a hairstyling show if there is one near you. If she doesn't seem very interested in hairstyling, you back up and start over again with another field.

Let's say she's showing some interest in cosmetology. She's reading all the books and magazines you got her and testing what she's learning by commenting on people's hairstyles. "That girl's forehead is too high for that swept back style. She'd look better with bangs." She is also starting to do different things with her own hair. That's your cue to move to the third step.

You let her try it for herself.

One way to do this might be to talk with the person who does your hair. Explain the situation to her and tell her you would like to pay her to coach you daughter while your daughter styles hair. If that turns out halfway decent, and it's bound to, your daughter is on her way. You can encourage her to continue practicing on other family members and friends, and you can start making plans with her to go to cosmetology school after high school.

As you can see, this is going to take a lot of your time, especially if you have to back up several times and try different career paths until you find one that interests your daughter. I'm afraid there is no shortcut. If you leave teenagers to find their own way in the mainstream, the chances of them succeeding and staying in the mainstream are not nearly as good as they are if you help them make the transition. If you are wondering how you are going to find the time, consider the alternative.

Keep in mind, as you assist teenagers in making the transition from the street to the mainstream, as you redirect their talents and abilities, that despite its dangers and maybe because of them, the street is exciting and excitement is addictive. Once teenagers have acquired a taste for excitement, they won't want to and won't be able to live without it. That means you will need to find a way to show them that life in the mainstream can be exciting, too. You can't simply tell them, "It's time to grow up. Life isn't all fun and games." The need for excitement is very real for teenagers who have been on the street, and if they can't find it in the mainstream, they'll go back to the street to get it.

Addiction to excitement isn't just a street thing. It happens just as easily and regularly to mainstream folks who have experienced the adrenaline rush that one gets from facing danger. You probably know some mainstream excitement junkies yourself. It started with a white water rafting trip. Then it was rock climbing or mountain biking and on to bungee jumping. Next time you talked to them they were taking up sky diving and planning a vacation in the Amazon.

If those activities are a little extreme for your tastes and budget, don't worry. You can help teenagers find excitement in more commonplace activities like skiing (snow or water), camping, snorkeling, deep-sea fishing, and riding the biggest roller coaster at the local amusement park. Even taking teenagers to see something they've never seen before, like a play, a ballet, a rodeo, the circus, or a big league sporting event can be exciting. If you can't do these sorts of things with teenagers yourself, for whatever reason, try to find someone who can. You'd be surprised how many people would be happy to help a teenager make it back to the mainstream if they just knew what they could do to help. I once asked a yachtsman to take inner city teenagers who were trying to get off the street as crew members when he raced his sailboat on a nearby lake. He agreed, identified several young people, and trained them. The teenagers couldn't stop talking about the experience and the yachtsman said it was the best time he'd ever had sailing. The point is teenagers who have been on the street need excitement, and if you want them to come back to the mainstream, you have to show them they can find excitement there, as well.

So that's the Streetwise Strategy. Establish a non-threatening relationship, impose the consequences of street behavior, and then redirect the talents and abilities teenagers are using to survive on the street to help them succeed in the mainstream. As I said earlier, it isn't easy, but it is simple—and it works.

8

Drugs, Gangs, and Violence

D rugs, gangs, and violence—the big three. The hot buttons. The mere mention of these words strikes fear in the hearts of most American communities. I've saved them for last because I wanted you to understand the Streetwise Strategy before I started talking about these emotionally charged issues. I wanted you to understand the Streetwise Strategy because that's what you use to deal with these problems, one teenager at a time.

I've lumped the big three together in one chapter, instead of dealing with each of them separately, because they are very similar to one another in nature. They are all street manifestations of mainstream norms. The mainstream in the United States is a violent, cliquish society that believes in using drugs to feel good. Drugs, gangs, and violence on the street are very much like their mainstream counterparts, except that in the mainstream, these behaviors are carried out within the law, and on the street, they are carried out without regard for the law. So it isn't the mere act of using drugs or joining gangs or behaving violently that is the problem. It's doing these things without regard for the law that makes them unacceptable. That brings us right back to the street versus the mainstream and the Streetwise Strategy.

I'm sure not everyone will agree with what I just said. In fact, some people may strongly disagree with me. These are, after all, very emotionally charged subjects. I understand this and don't wish to deny you your opinions or your feelings. All I ask is that you hear me out. I hope to be able to help you better understand what is going on in this country with drugs, gangs, and violence so that you can, perhaps, be less emotional and more objective about them and, ultimately, be more effective in dealing with them.

Let's start with violence. This nation was created by a revolution. Our history is a series of wars, the most brutal of which was the one we fought with ourselves. Most of our favorite pastimes are violent. If we're not doing something violent, like hunting or learning karate, we're watching something violent, like boxing, wrestling, football, and hockey—even auto racing—which it is generally agreed most people watch to see the crashes. Most of our national heroes are associated with some violent act in the course of war or sports, or with the portrayal of violent acts in an action adventure movie. Our films and television programs are so filled with violence that we had to set up a rating system so people could tell which ones weren't violent. We are a nation of superheroes, shootouts, and sudden death overtime. And just in case all that isn't violent enough, we created roller derby and WWF Smackdown. I'm not suggesting that everyone in the mainstream is violent or attracted to violence. However, ours is the only society in the world where you'll find a grandmother at a football game on a fall Sunday afternoon with a simulated cheese wedge on her head screaming at the top of her lungs for a bunch of three hundred-pound defensive linemen to "kill" a little guy with a ball.

This is not an indictment of the mainstream. I am not making a judgment here. You simply cannot expect teenagers, who have grown up watching the good guys blow away the bad guys on television, in the movies, and in real life, not to think that violence is an acceptable way to resolve your differences or get what you need and want. The system may say violence is not acceptable, but the popular culture says it is. And teenagers are much more likely to respond to the popular culture than to the system, especially if they don't see themselves as being part of that system, which they don't.

Should we accept drive-by shootings as the price of indulging our violent tendencies? Absolutely not! The mainstream recognized its violent tendencies from the very outset. We created our strongest laws, which carry the most severe penalties, as a means of both discouraging these tendencies and removing unacceptably violent individuals from the society. When I point to the violent nature of the mainstream I am merely stating a reality that has to be taken into account. I am not saying we should condone or condemn violence. I am saying we should use the laws we have on the books to help teenagers understand the difference between violence that is acceptable and violence that is not acceptable to the mainstream. The problems we have in this country with teenage violence are not about violence. They are about what behavior is legal and what behavior isn't. They are about the line that separates the street from the mainstream.

Next let's talk about gangs. What's wrong with wanting to belong, to be part of a select group of people who will help and support you simply because you are a member of their group? And is there really anything wrong with wanting to let the world know that you are a member of that special group? It doesn't bother us if a Shriner wears a red fez. Why should it bother us that a Blood wears a red bandana? Street gangs, you see, are the fraternal orders, the social clubs, the business associations, and the service organizations of the street. People who live on the street join gangs for all the same reasons that people who live in the mainstream join mainstream organizations. Gangs, like mainstream organizations, have a purpose and a hierarchy. Some are purely self-serving, others are geared toward social activities, some have a business bent, and still others have a sense of civic responsibility (such as protecting their neighborhoods from intruders). Their "colors" are their way of saying, "I'm a member of this organization." In this way, they are no different from the matching jackets and elaborate pins Mary Kay sales people wear. Their hand signs are part of the ritual that binds them together, and that ritual is no more secretive nor intrinsically destructive than the rituals practiced by organizations like the Masons. Since gangs usually can't afford lodge halls, offices, or meeting rooms, they meet on the street and "tag" the surrounding buildings and walls as a way of telling the rest of the world, "This is our place." What distinguishes street gangs from the mainstream organizations is the fact that the mainstream organizations operate within the law while the street gangs operate without regard for the law.

The existence of gangs is not a problem, nor is belonging to a gang a problem. It is the illegal things gangs do that make them problems. You don't get teenagers out of gangs by telling them not to belong. You get them out of gangs by giving them something more acceptable to belong to, something that meets the same needs gangs meet.

If you try to get teenagers out of gangs by giving them something else, something positive to belong to, you need to understand that you are going to run into an obstacle. You will need to be prepared to overcome that obstacle if you want to succeed. The obstacle comes after you have established a nonthreatening relationship, and after you have imposed the consequences of street behavior. It comes right about the time you are trying to redirect the teenager's talents and abilities from the street to the mainstream. That's when you find out law-abiding mainstream organizations won't accept teenagers as members because they were in gangs. This means that, if you really want to get teenagers out of street gangs, you not only have to work with the teenagers one at a time, you also have to educate the mainstream organizations that provide the kind of comradeship and support teenagers find in the gangs. You have to show these organizations why it is so important for them to let these teenagers in. And you have to show them how to help redirect the talents and abilities these teenagers have been using to contribute to their gang's mission so they can make equally valuable contributions to the missions of the mainstream organizations.

Next, let's talk about drugs. I don't mean medicines that help regulate normal bodily functions, like insulin, or that cure disease, like antibiotics. I want to talk about all the stuff we take just to feel good—like caffeine, nicotine, alcohol, or the diet pills we take that keep us from feeling hungry even though they don't provide any nourishment. I want to talk about the tranquilizers we take to feel calm, even though they don't resolve the problems that are troubling us, and all the cold remedies we take to relieve our symptoms that don't cure our colds. This is very commonplace and widely accepted behavior in the mainstream. Children learn it at a very early age. "Not feeling well? Oh, I'm sorry. Here, take this pill. It will make you feel better." If you're still not convinced, try this little test. What is the last sentence in this everyday dialog? "How are you?" "I'm not feeling well. I have a splitting headache." "Did you [fill in the blank]?" You got it didn't you? The missing phrase was, "take something for it?" That's what we do in the mainstream when we don't feel well—we take something for it. We take a drug to make ourselves feel better.

How can you expect teenagers not to think it's okay to use drugs in order to feel good when they grow up being told to do just that (which, by the way, is the only reason a teenager, or anyone else for that matter, uses drugs—to feel good). I know some people say it's the availability of drugs that's creating the problem and argue that we have to stamp out the drug dealers. Of course, a lot of these same people had a totally different attitude about drug dealers twenty years ago when they were trying to score some "weed" for the Grateful Dead concert. Oh well, times do change. Now these same people contend that teenagers don't want to use drugs, but unscrupulous drug dealers push the drugs on them. That just isn't true. It is the way mainstream tobacco and beer producers maintain their market base by pushing their products on teenagers with carefully devised multimillion dollar ad campaigns that tell teenagers smoking cigarettes and drinking beer is desirable adult behavior, behavior they should aspire to. But the drug dealer on the street doesn't have to push his product. He spends nothing on advertising and never gets stuck with too much inventory. Why? Because drugs are in such great demand. And why is that? Because they make you feel good.

Consider this. If I dropped a bloated, dead cow at your front door, would you barbeque it just because it was available? I don't think so. Have you ever heard of peyote, the little dried cactus buttons that produce hallucinations? People were experimenting with them back in the 1970s. Ever wonder why they never caught on? It's because they made you throw up. Teenagers, like everyone else, may try just about anything once, but if doesn't make them feel good, they won't continue the behavior no matter what anyone says. Drug dealers on the street don't have to push drugs. They just distribute the product and collect the money. There is such a huge demand for drugs, that's all they have to do. The teenage drug problem is not a supply problem. It's a demand problem.

"Yes," you may say, "but the drugs teenagers are using are harmful to their health." Please, let's not go down that road again. The teenage drug problem has nothing whatsoever to do with what is and isn't harmful to one's health. Marijuana is not physiologically addictive and is far less harmful than nicotine, which is very addictive and deadly. And too much alcohol will kill you just as dead as too much heroin. Yet both nicotine and alcohol are legal. And although teenagers can't buy them legally, they can consume them, which they do regularly, without adults making too much of a fuss over it.

So you see, as with violence and gangs, the problem isn't what it appears to be. The problem with drugs isn't that teenagers are using them to feel good. The mainstream not only condones that kind of behavior, it encourages it. The problem is the drugs teenagers are using are illegal. It is not about drugs. It is about breaking the law. Again, that's not a condemnation of the mainstream. That's just the way it is.

If you're having trouble swallowing all this, it's okay. I understand drugs, gangs, and violence are emotionally charged issues. I understand people have strong views and even stronger reactions to these subjects. Remember in the last chapter I said you had to look past the repulsiveness of street behavior to see the underlying talents and abilities that make the behavior possible if you want to bring teenagers back from the street alive? Well, this is one of those times.

Teenagers who use drugs, join gangs, and act violently have found a way to meet their needs. If you think about it for a moment, that's a good thing. We want our children to grow up being able to find ways to meet their needs. We know we won't always be able to provide for them and look after them. We want them to be able to take care of themselves. That's exactly what they are doing with drugs, gangs, and violence. They are taking care of themselves. They are "taking something" to feel good, which is exactly what we've told them to do all their lives. They are finding a place for themselves, joining with others, sharing with others, participating, and belonging, which is also what we want them to do and have taught them to do because we know none of us can make it through life alone. They are aggressively pursuing what they need and want and they are standing up for themselves, which, again, is what we want and encourage them to do. The problem isn't that they are doing these things, these positive things we want them to do, we've hoped they would do, we've taught them to do. The problem is that they've chosen to do these things without regard for the law. They're taking care of themselves, which is a good thing, but they've gone to the street to do it, and that is the problem.

And how do you get teenagers on the street back to the mainstream before they wind up dead or in jail? Establish a nonthreatening relationship with them, impose the consequences of their behavior, and redirect the talents and abilities they are using to survive on the street so they can succeed in the mainstream. In other words, use the Streetwise Strategy because that's what works.

This is probably a good time to remember that you can't make teenagers do anything. The objective of the Streetwise Strategy is to influence the decisions teenagers make, and you are not likely to do that if you don't have any credibility with them. I am bringing up this rather obvious point because, given the highly emotional nature of drugs, gangs, and violence, it is extremely easy to lose credibility when discussing these issues with teenagers. You may not feel the mainstream is a violent, cliquish society that believes in using drugs to feel good. I believe it is, but that's okay. You are entitled to your opinion. You are even entitled to share your opinion with others, including teenagers, provided you qualify it as your opinion. Many teenagers see the mainstream (if they recognize it at all) as a violent, cliquish society that believes in using drugs to feel good. It doesn't matter whether they are right about it or not. That's what they see around them. That's what they believe based on their life's experience—albeit limited. If you try to tell teenagers, not as a personal opinion but as a statement of fact, that drugs, gangs, and violence are evil and only bad people do those things, you are going to find yourself in an argument you can't possibly win. What's worse is the teenagers you are telling this to are going to think you are either ignorant or lying to them. Either way, you will lose any credibility you may have with them and any chance you may have to influence their decisions.

What you can talk about with teenagers is what is legal and what isn't. You can also talk about the consequences of breaking the law as it relates to drugs, gangs, and violence. They may not agree with you. They may even dismiss what you say with a cavalier, "Well, that won't happen to me." But they can't dispute the issue of legality or the consequences of breaking the law. They won't think you are ignorant or lying to them and you won't lose credibility with them.

Even more important than what you say to teenagers about drugs, gangs, and violence, in terms of maintaining your credibility and being able to influence the decisions they make, is what you do. Again, actions speak louder than words, especially on the street. You can't come home at the end of the work day and say, "Boy, I've had a rough day," then help yourself to a beer or a martini and not expect teenagers who see you do this to think it's okay to use drugs to feel good. Alcohol is a drug and you are using it to make yourself feel good. What else could they possibly think?

Along these same lines, you can't stand there in your Chicago Bulls (insert your favorite team) jacket and tell teenagers they can't wear gang colors. Wearing your favorite team jacket is your way of saying to the world, "I am part of a special group of people who support this team." So why shouldn't teenagers tell the world about the special group of people they belong to by wearing a distinctive piece of clothing?

And you definitely can't smack your son in the face for talking back to you at home and not expect him to smack some classmate in the face for being disrespectful to him at school.

So you see, it all comes back to the street and the mainstream. Drugs, gangs, and violence are the street versions of mainstream behavior. They are the opposite side of a single coin. The street is the mainstream without laws. Drugs, gangs, and violence are a part of both societies and have been for as long as the United States has been a nation. It is the law, the line that separates the street from the mainstream, that makes some drugs, gangs, and violence unacceptable and other drugs, gangs, and violence OK. This is the message you have to communicate to teenagers.

During Prohibition, liquor salesmen were the most notorious criminals in the nation. Once Prohibition was repealed, they became respected businessmen. It wasn't their behavior that changed. It was the law. It's that simple.

Don't complicate or confuse drugs, gangs, and violence with a lot of stuff that has nothing to do with them. These issues are not about morality or about conflicting research findings. We all believe what we choose to believe, and our believing something doesn't make it true. If you think of drugs, gangs, and violence, and deal with them, in terms of their legality, you will find them much easier to understand and much less frightening. Once you understand them, and your judgment is no longer clouded by your own beliefs about them, you can deal with them just the way you would deal with any other street behavior—by using the Streetwise Strategy one teenager at a time.

Let me relate a personal story that I think captures the essence of the Streetwise Strategy. It involves violence so I think it is relevant to this discussion. I've been telling this story to teenagers for years and it seems to help them understand what the Streetwise Strategy is all about and what I'm trying to do to help them. I hope it helps you as well.

My parents recognized that I was getting into a lot trouble in my early teen years back in the South Bronx and they were very concerned about it. So they scraped together every penny they could and moved out of the city to a small town on the south shore of Long Island that had been pounced on by one of the early waves of suburban developers. They meant well, but moving out of the city didn't help much. I quickly hooked up with other teenagers whose parents had moved to the same town to get them away from the city. We started our own gang and continued doing the same things we'd been doing in the city, which was mostly stealing and pushing other kids around.

There was this one kid at school, named Robbie, who wasn't from the city. He had grown up in that small town, as had his father and uncles before him. The men in his family had a tradition of being athletes. His father, uncles, and older brother had been high school football stars and wrestlers. Robbie was following in that tradition. Robbie was a gutsy kid. He stood up to me several times. I knew all the dirty tricks, but he was a trained athlete. We pretty much fought to a draw those couple of times and I respected him for standing up to me.

One day he came up to me and asked, "You think you're pretty tough, don't you?" "Yeah," I said, "I'm pretty tough." "Well," he said, "I bet you can't play football." You have to understand I had no idea what football was at the time. I had thrown a football around on the city streets, but I had never even seen a real football game. Nevertheless, not one to back down from a challenge, I said, "Can you play football?" "Yeah, I can play," Robbie answered. "Well, if you can play football, I can play football," I said. "Okay," Robbie said, "Then why don't you try out for the school team?"

Well, I did. And guess what? It turned out I could play football, and quite well, in fact. I made the first team and after a while something really interesting started to happen. I began to realize that I was still doing what I'd always done, which was push other people around. Only instead of getting in trouble for doing it, people would stand up and cheer. "Hey," I thought to myself, "this is a pretty good deal." That's when my life started to turn around. I crossed back over the line from the street to the mainstream and never returned to the street.

Robbie wasn't put off by my violent behavior. He saw past it. Even though he was only a teenager himself, he saw I had the talent and ability it takes to play football and he redirected that talent and ability from the street to the mainstream. I lost track of Robbie after high school, but I heard he eventually became a coach. I'll bet he's a real good one.

I'm sorry if you were expecting me to outline some grand social scheme or a megaprogram with megafunding that would solve the teenage drug, gang, and violence problems. I'm afraid there is no such solution short of changing the mainstream's norms regarding drugs, gangs, and violence. That, I believe, is possible and may well be worth doing, but I don't think it is probable that it will actually happen any time in the foreseeable future. In the meantime, how do we deal with the troubled and troublesome teenagers in our lives who are using drugs, joining gangs, and behaving violently? Limiting availability and access, making the punishment more severe, sermonizing— they've all been tried many, many times in infinite variation throughout our history and they haven't worked. What has worked with drugs, gangs, and violence is the Streetwise Strategy.

9

Making Choices

Thousands of people, maybe even hundreds of thousands of people, are using the Streetwise Strategy, or some variation of it, every day all across the country and they are getting positive results. They are preventing teenagers from dropping out of the mainstream, and they are helping teenagers who are on the street make it back to the mainstream alive. As I've said several times, the process is simple, but it isn't easy. You have to work at it in order for it to work for you. You have to be analytical, sensitive, imaginative, patient, creative, and thick skinned. Every time you talk with or interact with teenagers, you need to reflect back on the conversation or interaction in your mind and ask yourself, "How could I have done that better?" It is easy enough to say these things. It is much harder to actually do them. The day will most certainly come when you are talking with a teenager who has crossed the line or is considering crossing the line. You'll be trying to establish a non-threatening relationship, or imposing the consequences of their behavior, or redirecting the teenager's talents and abilities and you'll think the conversation is going well. Then, all of a sudden, the teenager will get angry and say, "You see, you're not listening to me again. You never listen to me," and storm off in a huff. Don't blame the teenager. Don't blame the Streetwise Strategy. Don't blame yourself. Play the conversation back in your mind and try to figure out what it was you didn't hear and why you missed it. Then try to do better the next time.

The Streetwise Strategy works with teenagers who are using drugs, joining gangs, or behaving violently. It also works with teenagers who are stealing, in all its many forms, selling their bodies, and running away from home. It even works with teenagers who are violating curfew, cheating on their exams, or just plain cutting school. It may not work with every teenager who has abandoned the mainstream to live on the street. I never said it would. For some teenagers, it may already be too late. If they've become a real menace to the people who live in the mainstream, they'll have to be locked up to protect those people from further harm or injury. There will be others who are too hard core and wind up dead or in jail before you can get through that shell that keeps them from feeling or caring. Fortunately, these teenagers will be the exceptions. The Streetwise Strategy will work with most teenagers if used consistently.

If I haven't convinced you by now that the Streetwise Strategy works, at least try it and judge for yourself whether it works or not. You can also talk to teenagers about the strategy. It isn't a secret. It isn't a trick. It isn't something you do to them without their knowing what you're doing. Explain what you're trying to do to help them and see what they think of it. The worst they can do is tell you they don't want your help. If they tell you that, don't be discouraged. Let them know it's okay and that you'll be available to help if they ever change their minds. There is absolutely nothing to lose by trying the Streetwise Strategy, and there is so much to gain.

If there is a troubled or troublesome teenager in your life right now, then you know how much there is to gain. You know what is at stake in a very personal way. But there are other reasons, besides the personal ones, to care about what happens to teenagers in this country, reasons to use and encourage other people to use the Streetwise Strategy. Recent media reports suggest that teenage violence and drug use are down. In fact, reports suggest crime in general is down. Does that mean fewer people are living on the street, that the problem is going away? I wish it did, but it doesn't. It means more people are in jail in this country, including teenagers, than ever before in our history, and that is frightening. The fact is, teen violence, teen drug use, even teen pregnancy are much more common in the United States than in any other developed nation. What does that say about us as a nation and what does that say about our future?

I'm certainly not the first person to suggest that our children are the future of our country. I may, however, be the first person to point out that our country contains two separate and different societies—the street and the mainstream. That raises the question, "Which of these two societies will our children carry into the future?" I am not suggesting that the mainstream is turning into an anarchistic, Road Warrior society. I do, however, see a risk of the mainstream's laws, and the values they represent, being eroded as more and more young people cross that line from the mainstream to the street following the example of their movie, television and sports idols, business leaders, and public officials. I do recognize the possibility that the mainstream in this country could collapse the way great societies in Ancient Greece and Rome did.

I see another risk, as well—the risk of losing the contributions these teenagers might make to this country and to the world if they drop out of the mainstream. I worry that the answer to world hunger, the cure for cancer, or the next great, life-changing technological advance is waiting in the brain of some teenager to be coaxed out by years of study and practice. And I worry about what will happen to that discovery if that teenager drops out of the mainstream and winds up dead or in jail. Will their contribution be lost for another century? Another millennium? And what impact will that loss have on the mainstream in this country? What impact will that loss have on civilization as we know it?

Think about it. What if there is a virus mutating somewhere that will eventually be able to wipe out all human life on the planet and the key to the cure for that virus is in the head of a teenager who is living on the street and is going to wind up dead or in jail before he or she has the chance to discover and use that key? Does that sound farfetched? It isn't. You can never tell what a teenager may ultimately be capable of doing. In fact, very few people actually start out doing what they end up doing. I know a young man who started his working life in an auto body shop. If you like the work and are good at it, that's a pretty good career. But he didn't like the work and he wasn't good at it. He chose that line of work because that's all he thought he was capable of doing. Eventually, with the help and support of his family, he quit his job at the auto body shop, and went to college. He is now a very successful and prominent physician and a lot of people are healthy and alive today because of what he did. What would have happened to those people if he had never become a doctor? It was a lot easier for him to change professions than it is for teenagers to move from the street to the mainstream. They need help and we have to provide it if they are to realize their full potential.

I believe the widespread and consistent use of the Streetwise Strategy by everyone who comes in contact with teenagers is what will turn the tide. I believe bringing one teenager at a time back from the street alive is what will solve the teenage dropout problem and ensure the future of the mainstream. I hope you believe that, too.

You are coming to the end of this book. Having read the book carries with it a certain degree of responsibility. You can no longer claim you don't know what to do about the troubled and troublesome teenagers in your life and in your community. I've told you what you can do. I've told you what works and explained how to make it work for you. That puts the future in your hands. You can spend more and more of your hard earned money punishing teenagers who break the law by locking them up. Or you can ignore those troubled and troublesome teenagers and watch the ranks of teenagers living on the street grow. If that happens, there will be fewer people to work in the businesses and industries that serve your needs and fewer people to pay the taxes that serve your community's needs. You can do those things and suffer the consequences. You have a choice. You can be a victim. You can do nothing or keep doing what doesn't work and then complain and feel sorry for yourself when the future doesn't turn out the way you want it to. Or you can make the kind of future you want for yourself and your children become a reality.

I urge you to do the latter. I urge you to look at every teenager in your life and in your community, not as an annoyance or a nuisance, not as an interruption of your plans, not as an embarrassment, not as defective or useless or unworthy, and certainly not as hopeless. I urge you to look at every teenager as the most valuable of all worldly resources because today's teenagers are our most valuable resource, and nothing less than the future of our society will be determined by the course they take. Will it be the street or the mainstream?

I know it is painfully disappointing when a teenager you've worked with or cared for winds up on the street. You worry, you cry, and you get angry all at the same time. You hope, then you delude yourself to keep hope alive. You start to think you must have done something wrong somewhere along the way, but you don't know what it is or how to make it right. Eventually, you may give up in despair and grieve. That's an all-too-common scenario. But it doesn't have to be that way. You can choose to make a difference in a teenager's life. By doing so, you create an opportunity to save that life. You become a player with a role in determining the future instead of a spectator watching it take shape from afar.

Teenagers continue to drop out of the mainstream every day. You may not be able to stop all of them from going, but you now know where they go, you know why they go there, and you know how to bring them back alive. I hope you will use this knowledge to help the troubled and troublesome teenagers in your life get out and stay out of trouble.

About the Author

After surviving his childhood in the South Bronx and completing his education, **Jose de Olivares** began his professional career as a police officer in St. Louis, Missouri. He walked a beat in the housing projects, worked undercover for the Vice Squad, was a member of the Riot Squad, and eventually became a plainclothesman in the Special Operational Deployment Division.

In the late 1960s, de Olivares returned to New York and joined the staff of the Nassau County Department of Drug and Alcohol Addiction. His innovative work in drug treatment and prevention caught the eye of President Nixon's Special Action Office on Drug Abuse Prevention and brought de Olivares to Washington, D.C., as director of communications for the National Drug Abuse Training Center. He later served as training director of the National

Center for Alcohol Education, director of training for the Minority Legislative Education Program, and associate director of the Job Corps Management Assistance and Training System.

In 1985, de Olivares founded Streetwise, Inc., to provide technical assistance and training to Job Corps staff and others working with difficult-to-serve youth. He became center director of the Detroit Job Corps Center in 1988, and his success there led him to be appointed regional director of Job Corps in Dallas, Texas, in 1993.

De Olivares is also a much sought-after speaker. He has presented his work at the National Youth Summit in Washington, D.C., sponsored by the U.S. Department of Health and Human Services, the Fairfax County Juvenile and Family Court Annual Training Conference in Fairfax, Virginia, and the first-ever Global Youth Employment Summit in Alexandria, Egypt, which was attended by 1,600 people from 120 countries.

In addition to his professional achievements, de Olivares is an accomplished horseman and a nationally ranked fencer. He resides in Dallas.